MW01289213

Warlock Asylum

Esoteric Ninjitsu

Esoteric ("ess-oo-ter-rik") is usually defined as "intended for, or likely to be understood by only a small group of people with a specialized knowledge or interest." In that regard there is a great deal of arcane, occult, and "hidden" knowledge, reserved for initiates of this or that sect or cult, that is seldom revealed to the general public. The reason most often given, in regards to these sects confidentiality, is that the information is so complex that "ordinary" people, those without years of training and indoctrination, would be incapable of comprehending the secrets of the universe. This is, of course, absurd.

The wonder of the universe is in its infinite complexity and the way the differences combine to create meaning and beauty. The laws that govern this reality must necessarily be simple, if for no other reason, than that they must apply equally on all levels of existence.

Hermes Trismegistus, a wandering sage of ancient Egypt, around the time the pyramids were being built, elaborated the Seven Laws of the Universe to a population that had not even invented the wheel yet. They were inscribed on Emerald Tablets, held in trust by the high priests of that bygone era to be shared with the people, so that they would understand how the universe works and their role in it. The Laws are not complicated. They need no real further explanation or commentary, although hundreds of books have been written trying to "explain" or expound upon them. The Seven Laws are:

The All is Mind.
Everything is in Vibration.
As above so below. (Law of Correspondence)
There is an ebb and flow to the tides of the Universe. (Law of Rhythm)
For every high there is a low. (Law of Balance)
Make a good cause, get a good effect; bad cause, bad effect. (Law of Karma)
The principle of Gender operates on all levels. (Law of Magnetic and Electric Energy)

For whatever reason, perhaps because he too suffered from the sin of feeling himself superior to lesser mortals, Hermes did not reveal two other laws known to the brothers of the Pole Star School.

What will happen in one's life is already written, but one must choose to be there.
(Law of the Interaction of Fate and Free Will)
All things are subject to Change.
(The Law of Inertia)

But, even these two are not beyond the comprehension of mere mortals. They make perfect sense, without the need for convoluted logic or mathematical certainty, and are easily demonstrable at any time. "Repeatability of a consistent outcome to the experimental process" being the test of science.

The "test of reality," however, is much simpler. It is the sense of touch. "The eyes can be blinded by the five colors, the ears deafened by the five tones, the mind confused by ripples on the pool of the subconscious." But, when you "feel" it, then you understand it on a deeper and more intuitive level. Look at a baby's smile. The joy in that face fills you with love. You feel warmth spreading all over your body. You want only to embrace and share that love.

By the same token, look into the face of a bear, or just imagine it. When you feel the fear sweeping over you, you know you are looking death in the face. That is what makes it real. "Being there now." Feeling the wind in your hair, the sun on your face, the earth beneath your feet. That is when you are alive.

The purpose of religion, the teaching and explanation of esoteric thought to the masses, is to "show you your tiger face." Namely, its purpose is to explain to you who you are and what your role is in society. The term comes for an old Hindu legend about a tiger who was chasing some goats for a meal one day. During the chase the tiger was injured and as she lay dying, she gave birth to a tiger cub. The goats had never seen a baby tiger before, so they just adopted it into the herd. As he grew, the tiger didn't do too well. His teeth weren't right for chewing grass, so he was malnourished and he liked to climb trees and lay on the limbs to sun himself. The other goats couldn't do that, so they were jealous. One day another tiger came along and was chasing the goats, trying to catch one for dinner. He found the young tiger hiding in the tall grass.

"What are you doing?" asked the old tiger.
"Hiding" replied the young.
"Why?" asked the old tiger.
"Because I'm afraid you'll eat me," said the younger.
"I won't eat you, you're a tiger like me!"
"Oh no..." said the young tiger. "I'm a goat."

Upon which the old tiger bade the younger come along back to his den. There he told him to eat some meat from an antelope carcass. The young tiger protested, "I can't eat meat, I'm a vegetarian." But the old tiger made him eat anyway, and it made the young tiger strong. According to anthropology professor Joseph Campbell, this analogy refers to the initiate being compelled to face reality and see the truth.

The next day, they went to the pond to drink. Before they did, however, the old tiger told the younger, "Look into the water and see the reflection of your face. Then look at my face. You will see they are the same. You are not, you cannot be, a goat. It is not your nature. You are a tiger, like me." We are not all tigers. But, we all need to know our place.

Concealing the Laws of the Universe, misrepresenting them, distorting or twisting them for a selfish purpose, to control the masses, who are "too stupid to know better or understand" is not the true measure of humanity. It is merely arrogance.

Esoteric knowledge is not meant for the few, but for the many. It is only restricted to the Few who wish to wield power over their neighbors by tradition and subterfuge. Stop letting people tell you that you are too dumb to understand or that you aren't looking at the "big picture." If they can't explain it, if you don't feel it in your heart, then it doesn't exist.

We are not a secret society, we are a society with secrets; that we gladly share with those who ask. May your way be as pleasant.

I remain,

Ashida Kim

The Sacred Text
of
Ghost Dragon Kotodama

Written

by

Warlock Asylum

Copyright © 2015 Messiah'el Bey

All rights reserved.

ISBN: 1511925906
ISBN-13: 978-1511925907

Contents

The Fountain of All That Exists

Life is the total sum of consciousness, where the result is the origin of the cause. We gave you these instructions in The Ivory Tablets of the Crow. Immortals do not count their age in years, but in what they remember. Remember?

We say remember, as forgetfulness dwells in impurity. Look at how perfectly the stars in heaven remember their course. The winds we feel are the waves of air in the ocean of life. How can you say that you are initiated and still speak in the same manner? Blasphemy is the only word that can be held in the fire. Life enters fire first and in the fire some things perish and others are born. The initiator of Heaven and Earth, arbitrator of destines,. this is the world of fire. Listen carefully.

Know too, that there are three aspects of the Mind of Existence, Heaven, Earth, and the Netherworld. Life begins in fire moving through each aspect of the mind. So it was, that when Izanami-no-Mikoto gave birth to fire, three aspects of the mind were set in motion and in migration, for in fire things are born and things perish.

Fire, however, was born in Heaven and just by its existence, the Land of the Living and Netherworld, were created in the ashes of life. Still, fire is an element and life is life. But, this is how life in fire exists. Life also exists in air, earth, and water. Now the three aspects of life, being Heaven, the Land of the Living, and the Netherworld, must pass through the four elements and this progression is found in the stars as the twelve spaces in the Heavens. Remember, these are the experiences of Heaven, Earth, and the Netherworld, passing through the four elements, predictable in memory. This is what purity means.

There exists something that is contrary to such environments, however, the spark of divinity, which must carry itself as a spirit of the five senses. And the five senses exist in the Land of the Living as they are. The five senses of the Netherworld are clairvoyance, clairaudience, clairscent, clairtangency, and clairgustance. These are the five senses of the Netherworld. There are many people who will study the awesome spectacles of the Netherworld without knowing its cause. In ignorance they will dream of an ungodly power and think of themselves as having attained such. However, in reality, they are pets on a leash, attached to an evil force.

The five senses of Heaven are love, truth, peace, freedom, and justice, Thus, we have five senses in three aspects of life, which equals the goodness of fifteen. Now, the mortal world is the world of twelve, a reality of conditions and moods. It is the conscious mind. Fifteen is the subconscious mind, the immortal power.

When the Initiate has reached the maturity of the pure waters they can bask in these realms by use of their words, the fire, and knowledge of a certain formula, as it appears in The Yi Jing Apocrypha of Genghis Khan. In order for one to have success in these undertakings, they must have invoked the Dreams of the Crow. it is in the process of memorizing these Dreams that one takes their oath to The Fountain of All that Dwells Beyond This World. Once memorized they can perform the Dreams one after the other in their true form

1. ☰ = Johuta = ᒧᖮ = Ancient Baptism =

2. ☳ = Amaterasu = ᒿ⟋ = Soul of Fire =

3. ☵ = Yuvho = ⧺√ = Zasosu =

4. ☶ = Nudzuchi = ᒷ = Ayaqox =

5. ☱ = Owatatsumi = ᖯ = Muh =

6. ☲ = Shamhat = ᑌᕂ = Fahmu =

7. ☴ = Xuz = ᒪ = Quekanuit =

8. ☷ = Sheba = ᑫᕂ᠊ = Ivuwh =

9. ⛤ = Nyarzir = ᒥ = Takamagahara =

16

The Sacred Text of Ghost Dragon Kotodama

In the beginning, the Initiate must cleanse their person by invoking the basic components of the Nine Dreams. Before the Baptism of the Ancient One occurs, as revealed in the Ivory Tablets of the Crow, it is forbidden to light the fire in the Stone Bowl of Eternity. The smell of Frankincense and Myrhh cannot be acquired. Nor is the Initiate of the Sacred Art of Ninzuwu allowed to light White Candles. None of these things can occur until the sound, shape, and meaning of the Nine Vasuh Letters have been invoked. Nor can any of these things take place until Incantations of the Crow are invoked and understood. None of these things can occur until the Nine Mudras and Mantras of the Armor of Amaterasu Ohkami are understood. None of these things can occur until the Eight Trigrams are written on the Stone Bowl of Eternity.

\

Opening the Celestial Gate

How can they perform tasks of magic, if they do not know the meaning of life? If an illness of such affects the mind, surely their lives will suffer. Know that what is often thought of as magic is not magic, but intercourse with the dead. There are many who claim the practice of magick, but have been deceived by foolish spirits.

Time is the greatest difference between Heaven and the Netherworld. Life is shorter in a world that moves at the speed of light. Its purpose is fulfilled at much greater speeds. It is said that one year in Heaven is a thousand years upon Earth, and a one-hundred thousand years in the Netherworld. However, it is also said that one year in Heaven feels like ten-thousand years on Earth.

Know that when the goal of the light is accomplished, it will fall into the Netherworld. Once it is planted in the Netherworld, it must raise itself up from the Darkness, so as to incarnate into the Land of the Living. Is it not written in The Ivory Tablets of the Crow:

"The witnesses of these thoughts are few. The mind must learn how to raise itself up and meet its reflection in the

realm of light. The mere reflection of this statement caused that which is no more to stare at itself in the light. Understanding these simple things is the basis of every creation."

This life can now complete the cycle of itself by rising from the depths of the Netherworld, depending if its actions are clockwise or counter-clockwise. The Law of Time is the Law of Initiation and all Time is Initiation, so it is the same with magick and sorcery. Magick is not found in rituals, magick being defined as the transformation of the Soul. There is another sort of magick, however, that is founded upon the employment of disincarnate spirits, or the loose fractions of consciousness, known as the elements. While these things do exist, they are not for the development of higher states of being.

Remember, that for one to evolve in being they must first understand the process of themselves. The Netherworld moves at a very slow pace. It is like a grinding of flour, as the wheel turns once every thousand years, and many years must be spent in such places. Comprehension of such a world is painful to the mind because it is not a place of flesh, but ghosts. The stiffness of this world is not in the weight of matter, but in spirit.

Now the Netherworld is a place of excrement for the Land of the Living. It is a necessary part of existence. Its mind is indifferent from the Land of the Living and if unchecked it will consume such a world, due to its purity. The Initiate must remember that the Netherworld is neither bad nor good, but pure. Both, Heaven and the Netherworld are two extremes of purity that function for the pure purpose of the soul. This is the Netherworld, a purifying force for the shadow of nothingness. Some say that there is treasure in the darkness. Perhaps, the Waters of Life can one find in its womb, but this is partially true. The Magicians of the Secret Lands know well this fountain, as it is positioned between Heaven and the Netherworld. The cleansing agent of life is in the quality of transformation that takes place in each room of the Dragon Palace, for here is where the Waters of Life reside. It is for this reason that the Magicians of the Secret Lands will carry fifteen into the Heavens, Netherworld, and the Land of the Living, for the result of forty-five, but also in the Dragon Palace and so these Magicians signify the number sixty.

The Heavens is a brilliant world, wherein matter is that of light, a fire of similar radiant awe. While the Netherworld is a receptacle of wasteful emotions, the Heavens creates impressions from nothingness. The relationship between Heaven and the Netherworld is the same as that of man and a tree. One must inhale what the other exhales in order to survive. This is the Law of Time, which is an initiation in itself. The real trinity is the phases of life, consciousness, a mortal drug. It is spoken of in the ancient records and conversations held between Izanagi-no-Mikoto and Izanami-no-Mikoto. The process between the Breath of Heaven and the Breath of the Netherworld exist is the Land of the Living, and this is all part of the Great Migration of Souls.

Heaven, like the Netherworld is a process of life. It is a pleasant dimension, but it must be understood that there are many Heavens. What is reserved for Man is an existence in either, Heaven, the Netherworld, or the Land of the Living. Yes, what comes into this world is here because of a clockwise motion and other things by counter-

clockwise movements. Take notice in what direction the mind is leaning towards in every action and thought.

Many have admired the Yi Jing Apocrypha of our brethren Genghis Khan, however, few know the actual shamanic formulae for these rites and how the Hexagrams are to be called. The Hexagrams can be called after the powers of the eight ruling trigrams have been gained in initiation. The invocation and initiation into these arts begins with Nudzuchi and concludes with Johuta. It is prepared in proper order for the sake of the Tradition itself.

When the Ninzuwu is initiating into this path, one trigram must be invoked per week and during this week its hexagrams are to be called also. Once the initiation has taken place, the Ninzuwu is obligated to call, or invoke, each ruling trigram during its time according to the Calendar of Mu.

The Operation of the Yi Jing

Now that you know well the Vasuh letters, there are other letters in the stellar realm, patterns of light and dark matter that will prove itself useful. And these letters of light and darkness are the Hexagrams of which we speak. First it must be known that the Temple of the Ninzuwu is different from the Temple of the Initiate.

The Temple of the Initiate is a sacred science also. It is neither a higher or lower science in the field of thine undertakings. Nothing in the Art of Ninzuwu is of a higher or lower order, so be anxious over nothing. There are even Initiates who are not Initiates. If an Initiate has not grasped that true magic is the ability to control, employ, and create emotions and thoughts, then leave them in silence, for they possess keys not of our initiation and can only open the doors to the realms of the deceased, Many are impressed by the workings of ghosts only to wonder about the ills in their own lives. Avoid the ways of the foolish.

The Temple of the Initiate is composed of the traditional mental altar, as found in The Ivory Tablets of the Crow. First, there is The Opening of the Sea Ceremony, and then The Soul of Fire is recited three times, followed by The Call of the Shamuzi. This is the Temple of the Initiate and useful for the works which precede this writing.

The Temple of the Ninzuwu is similar to The Temple of the Initiate, but can only be used by those who have made the Baptism of the Ancient One. Whereas the Temple of the Initiate is used in communication with the invisible and visible forces described in the writings of the Magicians of the Secret Lands, The Temple of the Ninzuwu is used in conversation with the said forces and also to employ many of these for various tasks. It is the Temple of the Ninzuwu that must be used to activate the Celestial Powers.

Now the formula for the Temple of the Ninzuwu is like that of the Initiate. The space of thy operations must be clean. Thy altar should be in the North place along with two white candles. Remember to burn frankincense and myrhh incense since one has taken the Oath of a Ninzuwu.

Clap three times and recite "Johuta" three times. The Opening of the Sea must occur. The Soul of Fire Prayer must be recited three times and The Call of Shamuzi must be invoked. Afterwards, the Sword of Ninzuwu incantation must be performed. When the Calling of these Sacred Prayers is complete, one must build a fire in The Stone Bowl of Eternity and perform the Cosmic Rite of Wutzki.

The Stone Bowl of Eternity must be kept as a metaphor for the mind and the mental fire contained therein. However, when the Initiate has reached maturity in the mystical practices they can follow along with the shamanic ways of the Ninzuwu themselves. In this case, exercise caution against the spirit of excitement. Purity is a must.

The Stone Bowl of Eternity in the shamanic rites of the Ninzuwu is a clean bowl with no markings except the eight trigrams on its outer side. When the Temple of the Ninzuwu has been invoked, and the fire made in the Stone Bowl of Eternity, one must call the powers of Nyarzir before all things.

After the Temple of the Ninzuwu has been erected and Wutzki called, the Ninzuwu must perform the Amatsu Norito three times then; recite the mantra of Amaterasu Ohmikami through the Nine Dreams, from Zhee to Shki and from Shki to Zhee. Once this prayer has been performed the Celestial Gate must be opened.

Within the Celestial Gate are the fifteen kami that created the solar system. They were personified by the Chaldeans as the goddess Inanna, and also Ishtar, after they left Asia and settled in the Middle East. This is the Opening of the Celestial Gate.

Izanagi-no-Mikoto, Izanami-no-Mikoto
Harae-Tamae (cleanse all)
Kiyome-Tamae (purify all)
Mamori-Tamae (protect all)
Sakihae-Tamae (may all beings be happy)

Awo-kashiki-ne-no-Mikoto, Aya-kashiki-ne-no-Mikoto
Harae-Tamae (cleanse all)
Kiyome-Tamae (purify all)
Mamori-Tamae (protect all)
Sakihae-Tamae (may all beings be happy)

Oho-tama-hiko-no-Mikoto, Oho-toma-he-no-Mikoto
Harae-Tamae (cleanse all)
Kiyome-Tamae (purify all)
Mamori-Tamae (protect all)
Sakihae-Tamae (may all beings be happy)

Uhiji-ni-no-Mikoto, Suhiji-ni-no-Mikoto
Harae-Tamae (cleanse all)
Kiyome-Tamae (purify all)
Mamori-Tamae (protect all)
Sakihae-Tamae (may all beings be happy)

Tsuno-gui-no-Mikoto, Iku-gui-no-Mikoto
Harae-Tamae (cleanse all)
Kiyome-Tamae (purify all)
Mamori-Tamae (protect all)
Sakihae-Tamae (may all beings be happy)

Kui-no-toko-tachi-no-Mikoto, Toyo-kuni-nushi-no-Mikoto
Harae-Tamae (cleanse all)
Kiyome-Tamae (purify all)
Mamori-Tamae (protect all)
Sakihae-Tamae (may all beings be happy)

Ame-no-minaka-nushi-no-Mikoto, Umashi-ashi-kabi-
hikoji-o-Mikoto
Harae-Tamae (cleanse all)
Kiyome-Tamae (purify all)
Mamori-Tamae (protect all)
Sakihae-Tamae (may all beings be happy)

After these a called into being, the Ninzuwu must recite the name of the Heaven Parent, the actual name of the Divine. This name must be recited through the Nine Dreams from Zhee to Shki and from Shki to Zhee in the following manner:

Ame-yudzuru-hi-ame-no-sa-giri-kuni-yudzuru-tsuki-kuni-
no-sa-giri-no-Mikoto
Harae-Tamae (cleanse all)
Kiyome-Tamae (purify all)
Mamori-Tamae (protect all)
Sakihae-Tamae (may all beings be happy)

After the Celestial Gate has been opened, the Trigrams can be invoked. First, the Ninzuwu must merge with the Vasuh letter associated with each trigram by moving it through the Nine Dreams, from Zhee to Shki and Shki to Zhee. Afterwards, the Ninzuwu must invoke the Dream itself according to that Dream's number as it appears in The Ivory Tablets of the Crow. The Number of the Dream is the same as the amount of days it was observed during one's initiation. If the Ayaqox is to be invoked for seven days during initiation, then her incantation must be recited seven times after the Vasuh letter associated with her, and so on.

Now when it comes to the trigrams themselves, they are to be invoked according to the Vasuh letter associated with each, and this can be done in the Temple, or by use of the Shrine, where the plant serving as an altar can carry the powers of the Trigram., but also by use of the mudra associated with the Vasuh letters in the Armor of Amaterasu Ohkami.

Once the Celestial Gate has been opened, it must be closed by reciting "kan-nagara tamachi hamase" three times, two bows, two claps, and one bow.

One the Trigram has been activated, the Ninzuwu must call each Hexagram that the particular Trigram rules in the days that follow. One Hexagram for one day. The Opening of the Sea must occur. The Soul of Fire prayer must be recited three times. Call the Shamuzi, then the Sword of Ninzuwu and invoke Hexagram's mantra three times. Close by reciting Johuta three times, and three clapa.

The Stone Bowl of Eternity

There are many who claim to have an affinity with the miraculous arts. How true they are to these things is a story for the Dead, for it is the ramblings of the mind that they confuse with magic. What many call magic today is the employment of the Dead.

There is no limit as to what can be gained from thy sacred arts. However, one should never use these arts as a means for acquiring material things, as these undertakings come from an impure mind. When one is truly involved in the work, the energy of the work itself, provides for every need. We are told in The Ivory Tablets of the Crow not to worship ancient civilizations for this very same reason.

The great cycle of civilizations has led to the practice of blasphemous arts by those who claim magical and religious purity. In such cases, one civilization is conquered by another and those who have conquered will surely consume the treasures of their victims. One of these treasures is the pure esoteric knowledge of an ancient world. Written in deep symbolism, this esoteric knowledge of civilization is taken literally by the nation that succeed the fallen one, so that what was once pure is now profane. Live without blame. Be diligent and obey the law of the land, in which you reside. Know, however, that these things are good for the purposes of civility, but be careful so as not to be entrapped by the world of mortal man and its undertakings. Know well, The Stone Bowl of Eternity.

The effectiveness of the miraculous arts is a gift for those of a virtuous heart. This is why it is preserved by the Ayaqox.

Real magic exists when the subconscious mind is pure. How can it be otherwise? The laziness of those who refuse to work on their own mind, in their lack of self-preservation, bring an evil to every good work. Think about it! How can the mind employ something useful if negativity exists in it? It is like praying for something that worries the mind. An evil intent can never create a benevolent action, even if the action is within the guidelines of the law and appears to be for the good of all. This is why purity is the first action in the Art of Ninzuwu. What benefit can water be to the body if there is just a little poison in it? Our experiences are shaped by the subconscious mind. Where is the purity?

Their foolishness is easy to recognize. They pray with an unclean heart, so their thoughts and emotions have impurities attached to them. The greatest power exists in the purity of the subconscious mind. Therefore, it is necessary that the mind be made pure. This is the Great Work. The influence we have over reality is based on how clean our subconscious mind is at heart. Unfortunately, what is often called magick is the novice ignoring the principles of purity and attempting to push forth an agenda that can only be accomplished by intercourse with the Dead. While such things may seem powerful, the people who engage in these spiritual acts of misconduct have to work twice as hard to produce the lifestyle of an honest man. Why not be honest in magick?

The pattern of life is also the pattern of the mind, the Great Migration of thoughts and experiences. There exists a Heaven, a Netherworld, and a Land of the Living. These too, are the Powers of the Mind. Yet, it is important to understand that Heaven is superconscious mind. The Netherworld is the subconscious mind, raw energy that has no discretion. It is the greater of experiences and akin to myths as the Beast that is subdued by a Man of Heaven. The Land of the Living is equivalent to the Conscious mind.

Within the Superconscious mind exists a Heaven, a Netherworld, and a Land of the Living. Within the Subconscious mind exists a Heaven, a Netherworld, and a Land of the Living. Within the Conscious mind there exists a Heaven, a Netherworld, and a Land of the Living. Within each of the three minds exists three minds and this is what the Nine Books of Dreams is all about. It is important to understand the workings of these things, as they reveal the Way of the Immortal.

Mortality is a process wherein the Divine Mind is not active in life. How can it be if we are impure? When the Subconscious mind is under the command of the Conscious mind, mortality exists. The Conscious mind is mortal like the Land of the Living, not seeing its origin, or the invisible forces that has reign over it. Random egotism becomes the depot of its existence.

Immortality is also a process. It is when the Superconscious mind takes reign over the Subconscious mind and the emotions that carry thoughts. Within the Superconscious mind is also the Dragon Palace. The Superconscious mind is the Sign of the Ninzuwu:

The Great Work of Nyarzir was given to the Offspring of the Ninzuwu that they may become Ninzuwu themselves and perform wondrous things at the proper time. It is in ignorance that many worship the Subconscious mind and call it magick.

Know that by the courage of Ame-no-Ukihashi-Hime-no-Mikoto, the Science of the Seven Ghost Dragons has been preserved for all purposes true and good. Let the faithful study these things that they too may extend their lives in making themselves ready for every commendable work.

The Seven Ghost Dragons

Why are those who engage in magick plagued with problems? Do not the results of their workings take on a life of its own? Feeding off of their insecurities, they slowly drift into a mindless fortress of reason. Still looking for answers, questioning the possibilities of death that surrounds them, are they not possessed with a will of their own? This is the answer to their questions about life, a will of their own instead of one from Heaven and Earth. This is how these experiences are created.

Know that the teachers of immortality are the Seven Ghost Dragons, gifts of Ame-no-Ukihashi-Hime-no-Mikoto. And these Dragons heed well the decrees of Heaven and Earth for they are the ambassadors of them. Understand the law by which they abide well. In Heaven, emotions orbit around thoughts like the planets revolve around the Sun. In the Netherworld, thoughts orbit around emotions like planets orbit around the Sun. What is seen in the stellar regions are all symbols of these principles.

And the nature of the planets and the stars represent the various hidden aspects of the mind, emotions and thoughts. Mankind can see and record these things for the benefit of understanding influences not seen. There is much benefit in such things, as the language of Heaven can be interpreted by these signs.

There is, however, the ghost element. Little is known about this science, for its name is often confused with the ghosts of the Netherworld, but this is not the case. Ghost, as a term, is often used to scare the novice, but its true meaning is unseen. Ghost Dragons are perceived by the layman as clouds, planets, and other forms of animated matter. These are also under the jurisdiction of Ame-no-Ukihashi-Hime-no-Mikoto.

And the Ghost Dragons are found in the spirits of words. Remember, in thy sacred martial art it is known that words are the clothes of emotions, orbiting around the source of each and every experience. In the beginning, an Initiate may find difficulty keeping the Subconscious mind pure. While they cannot control the influx of thoughts and emotions, they can control their words and use such as a guardian for the mind.

Remember the reason that most fall victim in their esoteric undertakings is largely due to their worship of fear, and pay not tribute to the inner Lord who sits on the throne. They beg for protection because they believe in evil and feed the very same force through such prayers. Virtue is the only protector of man .

During prayer, any word said in doubt is a tale of two forces and a habitat for fear to dwell. Take special care in the study and practice in the words of the Ghost Dragons. Now the time for its initiation is during the day, when the Sun is high in the sky and the Moon is present during the night. Prepare a clean place for thy work. It shall be a place in the North and cedar and pine incense should be burning, along with two white candles.

Know that it is the will of Ame-no-Ukihashi-Hime-no-Mikoto that the Ninzuwu cultivate the Powers of the Ghost Dragons. These things were set aside until the proper time of their revelation. Remember that there have been *many traditions of the mighty that has come and gone, even the most ancient of these has become as rotten fruit. Still, the workers of the rites lament a false sense of power and only the dead show up at the altars of deities who have abandoned this world. It is for this reason that their priesthoods have become corrupt and given to serve the desires of the common-man. Truly, they are ambassadors for wandering spirits.*

When the Ninzuwu is ready to accomplish the work of the Ghost Dragon they must Open the Celestial Gate in the same form and fashion as recorded earlier in this writing. However, the Trigram that is invoked must be the same as the time of the trigram and its ruler in the Nyarzirian calendar, for this constitutes the foundation of the rites for that time. Pay special attention! The Sign in the Nyarzirian calendar must always be paid tribute to before invoking the Ghost Dragons.

Once the necessary things have been invoked, the Ninzuwu must call the first Ghost Dragon, reciting its incantation while walking around the talisman, also known as its Sign, associated with the Dragon in a clockwise fashion. And the number of the Ghost Dragon is the number of times the Ninzuwu must walk around the celestial force.

When thy work is completed stare into the talisman and the voice of the ruler's attendants will enter the mind giving virtuous counsel, as these rites must take place during daylight hours at the times of the full moon.

The ruler's attendants are the energies associated with each trigram in the Yi Jing Apocrypha of Genghis Khan. These things are listed later in this writing. Understand, however, that each Ghost Dragon is a sacred spirit of each trigram. Close the rite by stating "Kan-nagara tamachi ha-e mase" three times. Two bows, two claps, and one bow. While the ceremony of these operations are complete, the Ninzuwu must read the incantation of the Ghost Dragon on the nights that follow. This the Ninzuwu must do every night until the Ninzuwu has reached the time to cultivate the next Ghost Dragon.

After each Ghost Dragon is invoked, the incantation associated with it must be read each night. And the number of nights the incantation must be read is the same as the number of the Ghost Dragon. When the number of nights is complete, the Ninzuwu is free to have intercourse with the next Ghost Dragon.

And these rites shall only be engaged by those who are initiated into the ways of the Yi Jing Apocrypha of Genghis Khan. Nor shall observation of the calendar rites be abandoned during the Ghost Dragon Initiation.

The Dragon of Johuta

Johuta means song of purification, for this is the Way. There is nothing in life that is to be worshipped. Only pay reverence to what is good and what is pure. While those who express fear, who believe in resisting evil, may appear to be sincere, they cannot see that it is by their belief that evil exists in their experience. Johuta, when cultivated, teaches that divinity is purity, purity of mind, body, and spirit. Nothing good can exist in an impure state of being.

Change begins when what is impure becomes pure and what is pure becomes impure. This is not a moral discussion as much as it is the process of how one principle moves from one world to the next. It is a cycle that is not to be judged. Remember, what is written in The Ivory Tablets of the Crow:

"Take what is not useful and plant it in a good place."

We are not here to judge the world, for we are a principle of life and only in purity can the principles of Heaven and Earth be understood. Every rite that preceded this work is a rite of purification, a purification of the mind, body, and spirit. This is the Way of the Ninzuwu.

Unforgiveness can keep one in a state of impurity. It is a cause of depression and sickness. Once the state of Ninzuwu has been actualized, such vices can easily be seen. Happiness is reaped by those who work for it. Happiness is pure. Happiness is the Way. There are times when you will see demons arise from words of truth. It may seem strange to the mind, but do understand that the only truth is how emotions are being moved from one place to another. All of this is made possible by the words we speak and how nature speaks to us.

Johuta is associated with the Sun because the purity of the Sun, being made evident by its fire, is the state of existence that has made life possible, the cause behind the principle. Purity is the light of the Goddess. What light exists in the Yin force and shines so brightly? Is it not the Yi Jing itself? It is for this reason that the number of Johuta is Eight.

Study well the colors of Johuta. Her skin is a purple complexion and she wears gold garments. Royalty is purity and the keys of initiation can only be shared with those who are pure. Know that our level of initiation is also a level of purity. Many will come in the name of a popular god, or some school of magic, whose purpose in the world appears to be pure, but its congregations are filled with impurity and people who hold more faith in fear than in love. They will defend every habit of negative thinking made possible. People of this nature can easily be identified by their belief in the world's destruction. It is a sickening sight to see such self-righteousness act out of gossip, predicting a coming doom and feeling good over accurate results. Fear is the only form of spirituality they will acknowledge.

Within such poisonous environments, however, are those who justify these unclean activities with traditions. They will make every excuse and cite various histories of the nations as a means of justifying their behavior, but the truth is very simple. Each and every Initiate is impregnated with a spiritual embryo. What is bad during pregnancy is *bad for the Initiate. What is good during pregnancy is good for the Initiate. It is a very simple matter indeed! What toxins will a pregnant women take into her body are those based on a desire of selfishness. Preserving life is an act of purity. It begins with keeping the breath clean.*

Now the colors of Johuta, the colors of purity are found in their esoteric understanding, though these representations can be seen sometimes in one's experience. The Initiate will experience sunlight in dreams. Purple is the radiant awe of abundant lifeforce energy, resulting from one's purity. It is the color of good judgement, royalty through shamanic-mystical practice, and the power of detoxification over our bodies. There is much beauty in purple.

Gold is the robe of Johuta. What clothes can purity wear? Is it not experience? Gold is the color of every successful undertaking. It is not success for the one who is capable of invoking such an experience, as it is for all in the experience.

Johuta is purity and the meaning of such things is obscure, but also that of the Heavens. The recognition of Johuta in the Dream of experience can be found in things that enrich the soul. It is said that Johuta cannot be found in an unclean space. There is no vitality in things that lack purity. Tiredness, day after day, is a sign that one must cleanse themselves spiritually. The Armor of Amaterasu Ohkami is useful towards such aims.

When the Initiate has experienced the Resurrection of the Dragon of Johuta their eyes will see things not seen before and hear what cannot be heard by others. The Initiate can

see the condition of life for themselves and others.
Remember, the number of Johuta is eight.

Once you have entered the Sphere of Johuta, the mind will
see that all is mind and experience itself is matter, a rock on
the plains of time. Glimpses of the Divine World will be
revealed in acquiring your true alignment with the universe.
Love is paramount. It is for this reason that Johuta is the
first of the Dragons that you must be resurrected.

The Dragon of Aixu

Aixu is the Dragon of Loyalty. Her face is night on one side and day on the other, as Loyalty is a result of seeing beyond the day during the night and knowing that during the day night will return. Wisdom is cultivated by observing our thoughts and feelings. Giving life to the spirit by seeing beyond one's reasoning. Many will inquire about the meaning of spirit. They will wonder if life exists in a world beyond their own. The answer to these questions is found not in logical conclusions, but in knowing that if thoughts are the stars and planets are the emotions that revolve around them, perhaps the invisible force of the universe, its intelligence, is spirit. The spirit is love.

There is also an unseen form of matter that dwells in darkness. These are the Dragons. Unfaithfulness is preparation for an unexpected change, a perversion of the Will. During the Resurrection of the Dragon of Aixu the Initiate will gain insight about the journey of Karma, often called initiation in the mysteries of mysticism. All initiation is Karma. If Man is a principle of Heaven and Earth, then a deity is a principle of Karma. All initiation is Karma. And those who are asleep in the Dream, are those who are ignorant that every Dream is a measurement of Karma. Humanity is not a Dream, but all that is perceived to be alive by Man is a part of humanity.

Now the layman will be convinced that Karma is a moral action, literally, having to do with obedience to some law made by a king that is no longer remembered. This is not

Karma or Morality. Karma begins in how we think of others. The judgements we pronounce in our own minds, concerning those we meet in our experience is the fate we have determined for ourselves. It is very simple. All is mind and when one uses their thoughts to condemn other aspects of the experience, they are destroying their own mind. This is how Karma is linked to Mortality.

Morality is remembering our relationship with the Divine World in each and every moment. Morality is remembering the presence of the Divine World in the forefront of our experience. The Dragon of Aixu has a face of both night and day as the night is our Karma and the day is our Morality and the night Karma. Remember, it is written that Loyalty is the progeny of both Karma and Mortality.

The Resurrection of the Dragon of Aixu must occur after that of Johuta. Aixu is associated with Mercury and an emissary of Sheba, the Wind trigram. Know that in the Resurrection of the Dragons each Dragon balances the one that proceeds it. There is a Lotus in the Resurrection of the Dragon of Aixu that teaches every Initiate the science of a native star.

The phenomenal world is nothing more than the physical manifestation of the mind of the Sun, a mere thought in the consciousness of life. Humanity is a star in training, but must obtain pure thoughts, those lacking condemnation, or perhaps they would recreate the same world that we are living in. The sacred number of the Dragon of Aixu is four.

The Dragon of Istu

Istu is the reflection of purity and the Dragon of Luck, a result of pure action. He administers the decrees of Heaven in a very subtle means, often working through subconscious suggestion. Istu is extremely tall, representing a form of consciousness that is far above the mundane things of the world, but it is the joy of life itself.

Many often question the Way of the Divine World. Is it really so? Istu will always answer yes. The spirit of the Divine World is expressed in a childlike nature of innocence. Its imagery is very enticing to the mind of a child. An Ancient One is not old, but innocent.

Innocence, however, is only one aspect of Istu. He is also the teacher of the Harvest. It is said in Nyarzir that Istu came into the phenomenal world as Tsukiyomi-no-Mikoto, a shamanic king who instructed the people of his kingdom in the ways of irrigation and how to grow food from the ground. What more is the harvest than a metaphor of the necromantic arts? The gift that Istu imparts is not only innocence, but awareness concerning the movements of the deceased. The Harvest is a time for ascension and this science is not the Way in itself, but it does affect certain occurrences in the phenomenal world. Yet, the Resurrection of the Dragon of Istu is mystical experience that is tranquil.

Remember that it is the Dream of Istu, which comes before the workings of the Iwuvh. Istu is a force that may seem obscure to some, but its purpose is to reveal the unseen influences behind experiences and how certain actions affect what appears to be an unrelated phenomenon to the thought at hand. Remember, everyone can hear what you think as a thought in their own mind. Istu is the revealer of this art.

Through the Dragon of Istu the Initiate gains a peculiar understanding of the Yi Jing Apocrypha of Genghis Khan. Istu is an emissary of the Dragon Palace of Owatatsumi-no-Mikoto and thus associated with the Water trigram and the Moon. Remember, it is written that Istu carries a scepter that contains eight heads.

Istu is the dream of romantic love, not to be confused with passion. The lunar energies of the Istu Dragon can enchant and attract that experience which allows one to absorb another. The sacred number of Istu is thirteen.

The Dragon of Viyah

There is a certain fruit that can be procured from the great teacher in Heaven. In effort of nonresistance are these things born and this is the quality of the Dragon of Viyah. In effort of nonresistance can one awaken from the Dream while living in the Dream. The illusion is in resistance, in taking sides in the same events that have occurred for thousands and thousands of years. If one is blinded by the current of life, in ignorance will they fight life itself.

The trappings of mortality are found in the resistance of life. While humanity is parented by the stars themselves, the senses of ordinary man create an indifference in understanding this reality. How the light is received from the stars in Heaven is in messages of resistance by the uninitiated and in messages of divine will for the initiated. These are the only two religions of man. Many who claim a path of magic show a lack of initiation for this very same reason, despite all the marvelous works they can perform in the name of the dead by the spirits of the dead. It means nothing, for they are still unaware of the processes of the subconscious mind occurring in themselves. It is in such ignorance that they will create a ritual for every ailment experienced by humanity. When the cure can only be found in changing one's mind. This is resistance.

Magic cannot be found in ritual and should not be associated with such things. Ritual is technology. Magic is doing. The cultivation of divine principles and their demonstration in our lives, practically, is magic. This is the fruitage of understanding obtained during the Resurrection of the Dragon of Viyah.

Viyah is associated with the planet Venus and is an emissary of Shamhat, making her an associate of the Lake trigram. She is spoken of in The Ivory Tablets of the Crow as part of the Thunder over Lake Hexagram:

"It was during this time that his passion was aroused by the Goddess Viyah. Yuvho employed a mortal king to build a temple for Viyah and himself, called Ioxna. Afterwards, he administered tasks to the Zhee, concerning Muh."

Viyah teaches the Initiate the path of nonresistance, a very rare initiation indeed. When one finds themselves in life confused over the misgivings of the craft, seeking to become what they are not, Viyah appears in the mind of the sincere truth-seeker. It is a teaching that many are not prepared for, but is as simple as letting go. The sacred number of Viyah is five.

The Dragon of Buhqz

Very few warriors have lived after encountering the passion of the Dragon of Buhqz. Within her passion is the fruitage of justice, for lust is the foundation of natural law. In its highest stage of development, lust is the foundation of a strong Will, the wand of iron. There are many, however, who are weathered by lust in its fiery context.

True passion is the art of war, overcoming conflict by means of enchantment. The Resurrection of the Dragon of Buhqz is a gift where the essense of the fruit with no name can be touched and eaten. Lust is the dimension clairvoyant ability.

War is no different than lust. Many worship the inversion of fertility, aimlessly worrying about the aspects of life. Cultivate virtue. When Buhqz took form in ancient times, she made every effort to defeat the mechanisms that seduced humanity into a way of error.

The Resurrection of the Dragon of Buhqz lifts the veil between worlds. It is said the hair of Buhz is like strands of fire, for this is her crown. Although she is regarded as a Martian element, the Dragon of Buhqz is associated with the Fire trigram and Amaterasu Ohkami. It is for this reason that her seven.

The Dragon of Koqw

Know that the foolish will question the need for virtue and actually believe that magic can be performed without it. This is perhaps true for rituals, rituals of vice, rituals of vengeance, but this has nothing to do with magic at all. Remember that our center of gravity gives us our own peculiar way of receiving light from the heavens, thoughts from the Heavens. If we do not discipline our minds, we will have to answer for all that is said in our minds.

Sometimes there are random thoughts that become perverted due to a lack of initiative in cultivating our own minds. How can one perform magic if they are not in control of their own minds? The mind must be cultivated before any act of magic can take place. Otherwise, the so-called magician's mind is only a tool for radical elements of the psyche to empower itself. They create an experience and the so-called magician feels obligated to invoke these powers. However, these very same powers are the source of the problem. They will isolate themselves from others under the direction of the negative sides of their thought process. Self-abuse will surely follow. This is why we cultivate the mind before any shamanic practice occurs.

During the Resurrection of the Dragon of Koqw, the Initiate's understanding will begin to see the process of the subconscious mind more fully. The height of Koqw is far above the level of common thinking. His long black hair reflects a profound understanding of the Footsteps of the Crow. Koqw is associated with the planet Jupiter and Yuvho, the Thunder trigram. His sacred number is 12.

The Dragon of Quf

Who can understand the death of the ego? Is it not said that the Dragon of Quf is the power of swallowing pride? Remember, it is written in The Ivory Tablets of the Crow:

"Before the Throne of Quf lies an eternal flame called the Oracle of Fire. The Oracle says that when Muh rises men will be filled with anger and ready to rage war against the gods, but man will not prevail, neither will the priests of men who have betrayed our sacred ways, the sons of Aho."

The spell of ignorance creates an illusion that power can be gained through ritual. These foolish murmurings are used to entrap the weary. Some hold faith in these beliefs and actually think of the ego as themselves. It is what it is. Until an effort is made to cultivate the subconscious mind, the work never begins.

During the Resurrection of the Dragon of Quf, awareness of the mechanisms of the false ego and its death in the river of fleeting consciousness becomes easier to recognize. Many will reveal the way of the subconscious mind. Yet, they lack the knowledge of how the stellar realms influences the mind. Others will have a planetary formulae, but do not have knowledge of cultivating the subconscious mind.

Know that the Dragon of Quf is associated with Saturn and the Xuz, the Mountain trigram. He is often seen with black lips and pale skin, indicating a knowledge of the primal language. His sacred number is eleven.

The Signs of Yukionna

There has been much written concerning Ame-no-Ukihashi-Hime-no-Mikoto in the steps and books prior to this knowledge, as she is often called Yukionna, the Snow Maiden. The Signs of Ame-no-Ukihashi-Hime-no-Mikoto are in all things. Is not the shape of snow seen in a star's light? It is the same pattern of plants and trees when viewed from above, and is one of the few semblances of the Ghost Element, the Mind behind the cause, existing and not existing in our realm.

The following Signs of the Ghost Dragons are called Yukionna for the consciousness that is embedded in them can only be recognized by those who have invoked these very same Signs. Remember that the Consciousness of the Ghost Dragon does not reside in this realm. Neither are there any emotions of this realm attached to it, with the exception of the varying degrees of love. These are the signs that existed before time, as the Sign and Power of the Ghost Dragon are those existing outside of time.

It is important that these Signs are copied exactly as they are seen. It is a unique technology that only the virtuous can ignite. It is a beautiful engagement with the spirit that allows one to transform themselves into a vehicle for a divine power not known to this world. Remember, it is written:

"Later, he constructed Seven Gardens on Earth, each resembling a city that exits inside the world that stands outside of time."

The Yukionna of Johuta

Trigram: ☰

Sacred Number: 8

The Yukionna of Aixu

Trigram: ☴

Sacred Number: 4

The Yukionna of Istu

Trigram: ䷁

Sacred Number: 13

The Yukionna of Viyah

Trigram: ☳

Sacred Number: 5

The Yukionna of Buhqz

Trigram:

Sacred Number: 7

The Yukionna of Koqw

Trigram: ☷

Sacred Number: 12

The Yukionna of Quf

Trigram: ☳

Sacred Number: 4

Resurrection of the Seven Dragons

True magic will always renew itself. This is something that must be remembered. And know too, that the Law of Kotodama was given to man from the stars. Letters are stars patterns and speech is the borrowed ability from the stars to proclaim fates. Speech is Kotodama. It is not a specific technique, but an understanding of the spirit that is clothed by a particular word. Remember, words are clothes for emotions and spirits.

These are the incantations for the Resurrection of the Ghost Dragons of Ame-no-Ukihashi-Hime-no-Mikoto, also known as Yukionna. The incantation of a specific Ghost Dragon is to be recited during its Resurrection. When the Initiate walks around the Cloud of a particular Ghost Dragon, in an attempt to restore their vitality, they must repeat the incantation of the said power.

Remember to Resurrect only one Ghost Dragon at a time and in the exact order must one follow the Way of the Ghost Element. Once the Dragon has been invoked, you must read its incantation every night before sleep until the Initiate moves into the rites of the next Dragon. The methods of such a Resurrection are as follows:

The Resurrection of Johuta

Aum-Hmu-Tuu uli joh yhi toci selu.
(moo-ah-you-mmh-ha-oot you-lee jo yeh-hee toh-she say-loo)
I am the light of the Sun in union.

Uli ama yhi uli ny arzir xiezhi uta amaja.
(you-lee, ah-mah, yeh-hee, you-lee, nigh, ar-zeer, zhay-ee-
zee ew-tah ah-mah-jah)
The Goodness of the Divine World through me shines.

Bnhu-Zhee Johuta! Bnhu-Zhee Johuta! Bnhu-Zhee
Johuta!
(whoo-nn-bee eehzz Joh-ew-tah! whoo-nn-bee eehzz Joh-
ew-tah! whoo-nn-bee eehzz Joh-ew-tah!)
Arise Johuta! Arise Johuta! Arise Johuta!

Aum-Tuu-Tuu-Phe gama nuwa uli xiwangmu maat.
(moo-ah-oot-oot-eh-ph gah-ma new-wah you-lee shee-
warng-moo migh-ot)
I now Awaken the Immortal Self.

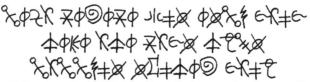

Nabu marama yhi aine zuhz tala uta muzi toci nunnehi
Ishtar zuho
(nah-boo mah-ra-ma yeh-hee iaw-neh zoo-hez tha-la ew-tah
moo-zee toh-she nun-nay-hee ish-tar zoo-ho)
Every part of my Body and Soul is in Harmony with
Divinity.

Aum-Tuu-Tuu-Phe gama anu zonget
(moo-ah-oot-oot-eh-ph gah-ma an-new zhon-get)
I now Clairvoyance enjoy.

Aum-Tuu-Tuu-Phe gama uli olokunsu yhi ataensic zonget
(moo-ah-oot-oot-eh-ph gah-ma you-lee oh-lo-kun-sue yeh-
hee ah-ta-in-sic zhon-get
I now the Harvest of Good Fortune enjoy.

Aum-Tuu-Tuu-Phe gama uli lewhu-aum-zhee yhi Johuta
hekate
(moo-ah-oot-oot-eh-ph gah-ma you-lee ooh-wel-moo-ah-
eehzz yeh-hee Joh-ew-tah hek-ah-tay
I now the Power of Johuta Resurrect!

ᕍᏋ ᏘᏋᐱᏒᏗᗑ ᕍᏋ ᏘᏋᐱᏒᏗᗑ ᕍᏋ
ᏘᏋᐱᏒᏗᗑ

*Bnhu-Zhee Johuta! Bnhu-Zhee Johuta! Bnhu-Zhee
Johuta!*
*(whoo-nn-bee eehzz Joh-ew-tah! whoo-nn-bee eehzz Joh-
ew-tah! whoo-nn-bee eehzz Joh-ew-tah!)*
Arise Johuta! Arise Johuta! Arise Johuta!

The Resurrection of Aixu

ΦΧΨΚ ΣΣ4ᴚY

Aixu Hmu-Hmu-Aum-Shki!
(ay-eye-zoo you-mmh-ha-you-mmh-ha-moo-ah-eek-hss)
Aixu, Come forth!

Nidaba yhi uli ny arzir Bnhu-Zhee
(nee-da-bah yeh-hee you-lee nigh ar-zeer whoo-nn-bee-
eehzz)
Messenger of the Divine World Arise!

Aum-Tuu-Tuu-Phe gama uli Phe-Hmu-Bnhu-Tuu yhi auset
tala mazu heka
(moo-ah-oot-oot-eh-ph gah-ma you-lee eh-ph-you-mmh-ha-
whoo-nn-bee-oot yeh-hee awh-set tha-la mah-tsu heh-kah
I now the Language of Heaven and Earth understand.

Aum-Tuu-Tuu-Phe gama camazotz uli arzir Aum-Tuu-
Aum uli evaki yhi tashnit
(moo-ah-oot-oot-eh-ph gah-ma ka-mah-zots you-lee ar-zeer
moo-ah-oot-moo-ah you-lee ee-vah-kee yeh-hee tash-knit
I now See the World by the Eye of Instinct.

The Resurrection of Istu

Bnhu-Zhee Istu! Bnhu-Zhee Istu!
(whoo-nn-bee-eehzz ish-too! whoo-nn-bee-eehzz ish-too!
Arise Istu! Arise Istu!

Aum-Tuu-Tuu-Phe gama namaka xihe
(moo-ah-oot-oot-eh-ph gah-ma naye-ma-kah shee-huh
I now know Telepathy.

Uli Phe-Aum-Aum-Bnhi muzi uli sojobo yhi uli takama
(you-lee eh-ph-moo-ah-moo-ah-whoo-nn-bee moo-zee you-
lee soh-jo-bo yeh-hee you-lee tah-ka-ah-ma)
The Dream is the Reality of the Subconscious Mind.

Bnhu-Zhee Istu! Bnhu-Zhee Istu!
(whoo-nn-bee-eehzz ish-too! whoo-nn-bee-eehzz ish-too!
Arise Istu! Arise Istu!

Aum-Tuu-Tuu-Phe gama mafdet toci uli Kunlun owoa toci
ryu
(moo-ah-oot-oot-eh-ph gah-ma maff-deht toh-she you-lee
khun-loon oh-wo-ah toh-she rlee-you)
I now Walk in the Astral Realm awake in Dreams!

ᚷᚱᛠᛏᚢ ᛗᛁᚲᛒᚢ ᚱᚥᛁᛁᚲᛉᛏᚳᛮᚥ ᛚᚷᚼᛜᚷ

Aum-Hmu-Tuu yhi mayahuel Hmu-Aum-Shki-Hmu
(moo-ah-you-mmh-ha-oot yeh-hee ma-jah-wel you-mmh-ha-
moo-ah-eek-hss-you-mmh-ha)
I am of Pure Mind!

ᚷᚱᛠᛏᚢ ᛗᛁᚲᛒᚢ ᚱᚥᛁᛁᚲᛉᛏᚳᛮᚥ ᛒᛖᚥᛉᚱᚥ

Aum-Hmu-Tuu yhi mayahuel vesna
(moo-ah-you-mmh-ha-oot yeh-hee ma-jah-wel ves-nah)
I am of Pure Heart!

ᚦᛖᛉ ᛋᚢᛒᛉ ᚳᚴᛒ ᚦᚳ

Soh gih uli wu
(so gee-eh you-lee woo)
Gentle are the spirits.

ᛉᛖᛩᛒ ᚳᚴᛒ ᛗᛁᚲᛒ ᚥᛒᛮᚥᛉ ᛚᚷᚼᛜᚷ
ᛖᚳᛉᛖ

Toci uli fah yhi aine Hmu-Aum-Shki-Hmu muzi zuho
(toh-she you-lee fa yeh-hee iaw-neh you-mmh-ha-moo-ah-
eek-hss-you-mmh-ha moo-zee zoo-ho)
In the altar of my Mind is Divinity.

ᚳᚴᛒ ᛒᛁᛮᛁ ᛉᛖ ᚱᚳᛖᛒ ᛉᛖ ᚱᛉᚥᚳᛮᚻ

Uli isis tz muzi tz yhi minuk
(you-lee eye-sis tss moo-zee tss yeh-hee me-nook)
The Miraculous Way is Way of Thought.

Aum-Hmu-Tuu toci pachamama Ishtar ny maat
(moo-ah-you-mmh-ha-oot toh-she pah-cha-mama ish-tar
nigh migh-ot
I am in Unity with Divine Self.

Bnhu-Zhee Istu! Bnhu-Zhee Istu!
(whoo-nn-bee-eehzz ish-too! whoo-nn-bee-eehzz ish-too!
Arise Istu! Arise Istu!

The Resurrection of Viyah

ᕼᏇᏇ ☉⌾ᚱᒷᑕ⊕╪ ᕼᏇᏇ ☉⌾ᚱᒷᑕ⊕╪ ᕼᏇᏇ ☉⌾ᚱᒷᑕ⊕╪

Bnhu-Zhee Viyah! Bnhu-Zhee Viyah! Bnhu-Zhee Viyah!
(whoo-nn-bee eehzz Vee-yah! whoo-nn-bee eehzz Vee-yah!
whoo-nn-bee eehzz Vee-yah!)
Arise Viyah! Arise Viyah! Arise Viyah!

ᏇᏋᎯᕼᐯ ╪ᚠ ᒷᑕ╪⌾ ᏇᏋᏇᏇ

Aum-Hmu-Tuu hu yhi ny Aum-Zhee-Bnhu
(moo-ah-you-mmh-ha-oot whoo yeh-hee nigh moo-ah-eehzz-
whoo-nn-bee)
I am Vessel of Divine Love!

ᏇᏋᎯᏇᎯᐯᐯᏇᑊ Ⴥ╪ᚦ ⌾⊕╪ ᕮ⊕Ⴥᚦᕮ ⊕⊕⊕⊕ ᕮᏇ☉

Aum-Tuu-Tuu-Phe she iah zaso tala zir
(moo-ah-oot-oot-eh-ph shee eey-ah zha-soh tha-la zeer
I attract Good Friends and Family!

ᏇᏋᎯᏇᎯᐯᐯᏇᑊ ᕽᏇ⊕⌾⊕ ჅᚦᚦᏇᏇ ⊕ᏇᏇᏇ
ᏇᏇᏇᏇ⊕ ⌾Ⴥ╪⊕⊕☉ ᕽᏇᏇᏇ╪

Aum-Tuu-Tuu-Phe gama sekinek toci nunnehi Ishtar lucxh
(moo-ah-oot-oot-eh-ph gah-ma say-key-nec toh-she nun-
nay-hee ish-tar loo-sigh)
I now Live in Harmony with Nature.

ᕼᏇᏇ ☉⌾ᚱᒷᑕ⊕╪ ᕼᏇᏇ ☉⌾ᚱᒷᑕ⊕╪ ᕼᏇᏇ ☉⌾ᚱᒷᑕ⊕╪

Bnhu-Zhee Viyah! Bnhu-Zhee Viyah! Bnhu-Zhee Viyah!
(whoo-nn-bee eehzz Vee-yah! whoo-nn-bee eehzz Vee-yah!
whoo-nn-bee eehzz Vee-yah!)
Arise Viyah! Arise Viyah! Arise Viyah!

The Resurrection of Buhqz

Bnhu-Zhee Buhqz! Bnhu-Zhee Buhqz! Bnhu-Zhee Buhqz!
(whoo-nn-bee eehzz Boo-heh-cuz! whoo-nn-bee eehzz Boo-
heh-cuz! whoo-nn-bee eehzz Boo-heh-cuz!)
Arise Buhqz! Arise Buhqz! Arise Buhqz!

Zaramama yhi zorya Aum-Tuu-Tuu-Phe freya
(Za-rah-ma-ma yeh-hee zore-yah moo-ah-oot-oot-ehph fray-
yah)
Lady of Honor I Praise!

Aine Inanna muzi eos Ishtar orisha
(iaw-neh eh-nah-nah moo-zee ee-oh-ss ish-tar ore-ree-sha)
My Life is Blessed with Abundance.

Ishtar ni Aum-Zhee-Bnhu Aum-Tuu-Tuu-Phe dharma uli
krystz
(ish-tar nigh moo-ah-eehzz-whoo-nn-bee moo-ah-oot-oot-
eh-ph thar-mah you-lee chris-tez)
With Divine Love I conquered the false ego.

Ishtar Anahit toci uli ny-arzir aho olel
(ish-tar an-nah-het toh-she you-lee nigh-ar-zeer ah-ho oh-lel)
With faith in the Divine World evil departs.

Uli joh yhi Amaterasu Ohkami adahes aine uta
(you-lee jo yeh-hee ah-ma-te-ra-su-oh-ka-mee ah-da-es iaw-neh ew-tah)
The Light of Amaterasu Ohkami protects my Soul!

Bnhu-Zhee Buhqz! Bnhu-Zhee Buhqz! Bnhu-Zhee Buhqz!
(whoo-nn-bee eehzz Boo-heh-cuz! whoo-nn-bee eehzz Boo-heh-cuz! whoo-nn-bee eehzz Boo-heh-cuz!)
Arise Buhqz! Arise Buhqz! Arise Buhqz!

The Resurrection of Koqw

Bnhu-Zhee Koqw aine vesna muzi kaatakilla nanweu
(whoo-nn-bee-eehzz koh-qew iaw-neh ves-nah moo-zee
kah-ah-ta-kill-la nan-weigh)
Arise Koqw! My Heart is without worry!

Shki-Phe-Nzu-Nzu-Phe muzi uli ixchel yhi aine Shki-Aum-
Phe-Aum
(eek-hss-eh-ph-ooh-zz-nn-ooh-zz-nn-eh-ph moo-zee you-lee
iss-chel yeh-hee iaw-neh eek-hss-moo-ah-eh-ph-moo-ah)
Happiness is the Foundation of my experience.

Uli Shki-Zhee-Zhee yhi sharra itu akna uta eos
(you-lee eek-hss-eehzz-eehzz yeh-hee shar-rah-ee-too ack-
nah ew-tah ee-oh-ss
The Sphere of Prosperity has me blessed!

Aum-Tuu-Tuu-Phe maharu dhatri
(moo-ah-oot-oot-eh-ph ma-ha-roo tha-tree
I receive Virtue!

Aum-Tuu-Tuu-Phe maharu sekhmet
(moo-ah-oot-oot-eh-ph ma-ha-roo sek-mhet)
I receive Honesty!

Aum-Tuu-Tuu-Phe maharu Aum-Hmu-Hmu tala orisha
(moo-ah-oot-oot-eh-ph ma-ha-roo moo-ah-you-mmh-ha-you-
mmh-ha tha-la or-ree-sha)
I receive Joy and Abundance!

Aum-Tuu-Tuu-Phe thor aine shiva ki ny
(moo-ah-oot-oot-eh-ph th-ore iaw-neh shee-va kee nigh)
I accept my Heritage as Divine!

Bnhu-Zhee Koqw aine vesna muzi kaatakilla nanweu
(whoo-nn-bee-eehzz koh-qew iaw-neh ves-nah moo-zee
kah-ah-ta-kill-la nan-weigh)
Arise Koqw! My Heart is without worry!

The Resurrection of Quf

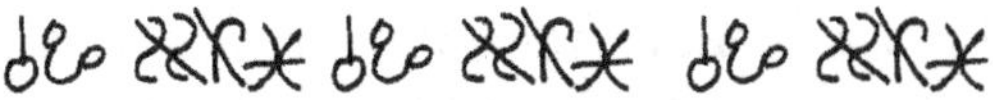

ᗫℓᗏ ℵᛝℝᚷ ᗫℓᗏ ℵᛝℝᚷ ᗫℓᗏ ℵᛝℝᚷ

Bnhu-Zhee Quf Bnhu-Zhee Quf Bnhu-Zhee Quf
(whoo-nn-bee eehzz koof whoo-nn-bee eehzz koof whoo-
nn-bee eehzz koof)
Arise Quf! Arise Quf! Arise Quf!

�96ᐰᛝᚷᘜᘔ ᚛ᕵᛩᚋᚋ᚛ᐧᕘᚋᚋ᚛ᕵᛩᕁᛞ ᘜᐰᚋ᚛ᕵ

Aum-Tuu-Tuu-Phe Honshazeshonen zuho
(moo-ah-oot-oot-eh-ph hon-sha-zay-show-nen zoo-ho
I radiate Divinity!

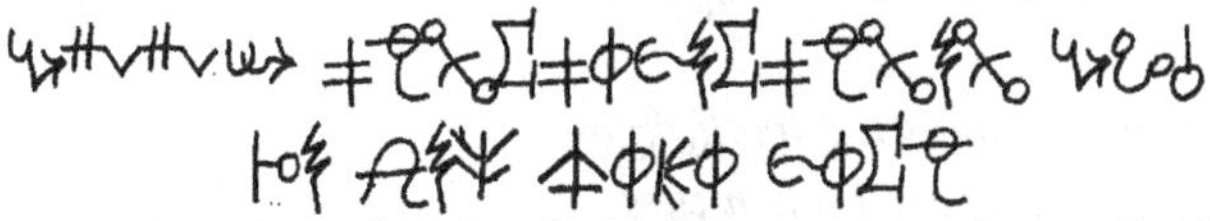

�96ᐰᛝᚷᘜᘔ ᚛ᕵᛩᚋᚋ᚛ᐧᕘᚋᚋ᚛ᕵᛩᕁᛞ ᘔᘔℓᗏ
ᛏᛞᚍ ᚕᕵᛪ ᐱᕘᛕᕘ ᚋᕘᚊᕵ

Aum-Tuu-Tuu-Phe Honshazeshonen Aum-Zhee-Bnhu de
jex tala zaso
(moo-ah-oot-oot-eh-ph hon-sha-zay-show-nen deh jex-xch
tha-la zha-soh
I radiate Love to Enemies and Friends!

ᘔᘠℓᛝᚋ ᚜ ᚕᗏᛜᛩᗏᚋᘜᚷᐧᛕ

Aum-Hmu-Tuu el ninzuwu
(moo-ah-you-mmh-ha-oot ehl nen-zoo-woo
I am a Ninzuwu (divine being)!

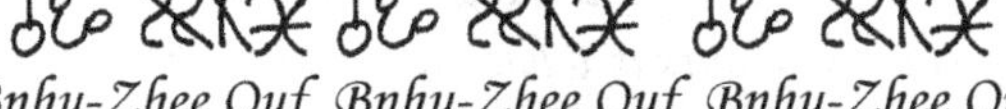

ᗫℓᗏ ℵᛝℝᚷ ᗫℓᗏ ℵᛝℝᚷ ᗫℓᗏ ℵᛝℝᚷ

Bnhu-Zhee Quf Bnhu-Zhee Quf Bnhu-Zhee Quf
(whoo-nn-bee eehzz koof whoo-nn-bee eehzz koof whoo-
nn-bee eehzz koof)
Arise Quf! Arise Quf! Arise Quf!

The Origin of The Ghost Element

These instructions are duly prepared for the worthy. In a very simple observation, the Initiate can ascertain that a great majority of magicians are not enlightened. It is so that even what is called magic is not magical, but an addiction to nocturnal hallucinations and wandering spirits.

Unscientific phenomena can be found in every aspect of the phenomenal world. And when the invisible is made manifest, the ignorant will ponder over such things as a result of magic, but not know its meaning. Is not confusion the result of wandering spirits?

One who knows the work, knows the work! And the work will continue even when these signs occur. There is some benefit in the study of these things. However, one must not be overtaken by these hauntings of the mind. It can only be said that if it is revealed, but is not known, should not the question be asked as to why a spirit would cast its pearls before swine? Perhaps, it is a vision obtained while one is standing unknowingly in the subconscious mind?

True magic, along with its aim, is very simple. We are to observe our thoughts and emotions, for these are actions as well. Pursue virtue by the use of repetition of certain words when the mind and heart is being bombarded with useless ideas, or fits of worry. Knowing that our inner and outer emotions and thoughts is what creates an experience, we now replace a useless sentence with what is useful. This is magic! This is simplicity!

If we are to receive the emotion of a negative situation and allow it to possess us, is it not so that we have left Heaven in this same justified action? The world is a test! Would it perhaps not be better for wandering spirits to present magic to the public as something it isn't? Maybe, what we call magic is the key to enslavement. There is as much magic in the world as there is religion, so much so, that it is safe to say that magic and religion is the world's first couple. Such foolishness can be avoided by remembering oneself as the reason behind the cause. It is for this reason that the Ninzuwu are described as Magicians of the Yi Jing.

Change, as a foundation, can be just as dense as solid ground when the reason is aware that it is standing behind the cause in an awakened state of consciousness. The Ghost Element is the reason behind the cause. It is the consciousness of sex itself once it has become self-aware. It is sex that creates and destroys. It is sex that is the reason behind the functions of Heaven and Earth. It is the principle of attraction between the yin and the yang. In awareness it is understood. It is the Ghost Element.

The reason behind the cause is sex, the Ghost Element. It is a form of consciousness that should not be confused with lust, but the desire of the cause itself. Time is a mere shadow of sexual consciousness.

Our work as Ninzuwu is the primordial marriage of the Yin and Yang Realms in life in order to become whole. This is a knowledge that has escaped many who claim enlightenment.

Bushido

These are the Seven Virtues of the Samurai, which must be incorporated in the Great Work. It is important that we incorporate this moral code in all our undertakings.

Morality 義

The common-folk draw emotions and thoughts from their life experiences. They are the sum of what they remember, also their culture, and their zodiac sign. During the course of initiation, the Initiate draws emotions and thoughts from nature and the celestial bodies themselves. After having irrigated the subconscious mind, what is absorbed is received in goodness. Morality is the result of our spiritual work. This fact cannot be escaped.

Some may claim to be of a superior morality and may even boast of titles that support such. This sort of morality, however, is as simple as wearing a garment, for this is what their morality truly is. When the doors are closed and nobody is looking their emotions and thoughts are just as diabolical as society's worst criminals. A morality that is received from Heaven would not allow one to entertain the mind with things that are corrupt. Bushido is really the cultivation of the subconscious mind. This is Shinto.

Man has to answer for every emotion and thought that passes through his being, as all of these things constitute an action, whether good or evil. Morality, in the true sense of the term, is never logical. Logic is a religion in itself. It is a religion where the answer is always right, but since the emotional being is never cultivated, neither is there a requirement for such in the world of logic, a man will perform what he claims to hate in public. This is the religion of logic. What makes sense is put before what is moral in the religion of logic. Unfortunately, the religion of logic is very popular among the common-folk.

People will say whatever makes them look good in front of other people. This is the religion of logic. Meanwhile, these same individuals will abuse a child, if it so pleases them. All of this is due to a lack of having cultivated the subconscious mind.

Morality is a vehicle of Heaven and Earth. The shaman is the standard of what is exemplified in society. There were many ancient nations that would not allow a king to sit upon a throne if he was not initiated into a right that would enable him to understand and speak with the planets and stars. Our morality is determined by how we cultivate ourselves spiritually.

Courage 勇

The spirit can only act on what it knows emotionally. Courage is not based on logic, but is a result of faith. Fear is the result of a lack of faith in the Divine World. Fear is having faith in what is evil. Many people who claim a form of righteousness worship both good and evil for this very same reason.

Our thoughts are visualizations and when we are consumed by the demonic force of fear, we may perhaps give way to worry. How can one claim to be a worker of good while having intercourse with the emotional quality that is found in evil?

Yes, the wandering spirits have designed a perfect scheme for such things. It is so that the reports of negative events, though few, take prominence over the majority of good that humankind is performing. If we participate in the foolishness of becoming consumed with these very same negative reports, then we are agents of an evil force. While it may appear that we are doing good, but to invoke fear in ourselves and in those we communicate with, is to rob them from the true joys of life. This is also the way of the common-folk.

Courage can only be enacted by the fearless, those who have unwavering faith in the Divine World. It is foolish to think that we are immune to unforeseen occurrences. However, it is foolish to exercise faith in these things by worrying, which is another form of prayer.

Courage is the result of true morality, as one understands their place in the universe, the more they are aware of the will of the greater good in regards to the evolution of mankind. When a child learns his parent's schedule, they no longer cry when they see their mother and father leave the house. It is the same with man's place in the universe.

Courage is the freedom to enact one's true will. And one's true will is within the Mind of Heaven and Earth. All of these things come into being as a result of the Ghost Element.

Benevolence 仁

When the process of the subconscious mind is understood, benevolence and mercy will dictate how we deal with others in our experience. Remember, the spark of life that is the cause of all things is in the world of man. It resides in every human being. People who harbor resentment against humanity are not aligned with their own process.

The subconscious mind is non-local. Therefore, the judgments we make about others in our minds can be accessed by anyone having a subconscious mind, especially those whom we meet face to face. Benevolence is not a physical action or even a kind word. It is one motion. Our emotions, thoughts, and finally our actions must work in agreement. Achieving this state of being is the goal of the true work, and then, the true work begins.

Whatever negative thoughts we hold of someone in our minds, our criticisms, let them be replaced by visualizations of mercy. This is how mercy is connected to benevolence. Putting our egos aside by the constant use of mantras and simple thought replacement is the good work. The battle of good and evil is a process in life that we must face before life begins.

Respect 礼

The fight of the Ninzuwu is never personal, but for the will of Heaven and Earth. Respect all life. The true warrior sees the adverse mind and its hauntings. Still, it must be remembered that an evil action is not evil in the minds of an evildoer, but an understanding of their own good.

Therefore, we must let those who are subjects of the Divine World take the lead in the disposal of evil. Respect all life.

It is truly evil for a person, in effort to evade their own issues, to make up a good and evil dichotomy and act as its judge. This is another religion of the uninitiated; creating good and evil dichotomies and judging the better of the two, in government, and in the lives of others. These are the works of the lazy man. It is an act of avoiding one's own evils and replacing them with making an opinion about an experience that they are not connected with personally. Their disrespect for life blinds them from their own evil.

Respect all life, for all life is a mirror of the subconscious mind. This is where the learning of the esoteric values found in nature begins. When we cultivate the subconscious mind, we our cultivating and nourishing all that exists in our experience. We respect ourselves by respecting life around us.

Honesty　誠

Honesty is the Bride of Heaven. There is joy in honesty for it breeds the way of happiness. Happiness is the natural state of humanity free from negative enslavement. When happiness is lost, sickness enters our being. As a result, we scramble between thoughts trying to find our place in life. An unhappy mind cannot focus. Dishonesty is the result of a lack of focus.

In order for us to begin the cultivation of the subconscious mind, we must be honest with ourselves. We cannot make *excuses for our erring habits. We should observe these things and use the tools we have to overcome them.*

Do not allow yourselves to be influenced by the whims of those who are not in the work. Honesty can be displayed by all, but is a definite sign of those who are in the work.

Honor 名誉

Know that the world will always be the sum of its collective consciousness. What some call demons are nothing more than a man that is plagued by his own thoughts. It is the same for a community, a nation, and the world of man.

There is a great temptation to return evil for evil, but such things are the work of the ignorant and a device of wandering spirits. When someone offends us, or makes an unnecessary critical statement about our character, it is easy for the unlawful to return this negative energy back to the antagonist. However, one must absorb this poisonous energy into their own system in order for them to return the hate that they have been delivered. Instead of one person being affected by the disease of negative energy, it has infected two people and this is how the disorder of the world is. Therefore, it is important to apply what is written in The Ivory Tablets of the Crow:

"Just take what is not useful and plant it in a good place. This is the only choice you have."

When someone deals you an evil hand, return their evil with good, as it is a shield against being infected by negative energy. It is the only choice you have. Never lose your divine status by entering and suffering from the ranks of resentment.

Now imagine if one of the common-folk, who hasn't learned the mechanisms of the subconscious mind or how our process of thinking creates our reality in its finest detail, decides they want to become a magician. Since they are not trained in the science of the subconscious mind, their work, if it can even be called such, is centered on amplifying and satisfying their poisonous mind. Their belief that they are a magician is the very thing that keeps them from recognizing the bondage that they are under. Yet, it is a perfect vehicle for allowing negative emotions to develop and enter our world. It can even be said that if such a person was a black magician, they are at least conscious of their own mind though they cannot see its infection. The common-folk posing as a magician is worse than black magic itself. The true work is not only cultivating our mental processes, but maintaining alignment with the will of Heaven and Earth.

Loyalty　忠義

Loyalty is the cause of enlightenment. Our obligation to life is to love one another and this love is given to man from nature freely. Therefore, the workers of nature are under the obligation of love. It is not a forced infatuation, but an obligation that is made by choice, for what is divine is love.

Divinity is all around us. Divinity is life and life in an advanced stage. Look at how much beauty comes with knowing. Loyalty to the cause of life is mere immortality.

The Rites of Forgiveness

It is most necessary that the Ninzuwu always maintains the practices of purity day after day. Perhaps the uninitiated may complain about these things, seeking a reward while living in a state of debauchery. Remember, that no good energy can inhabit an unclean place.

Are we not spirits in the flesh? And the body has only the task of work. The Priestesses of Old would often say that work is a gift from the Divine World. We are to use what we have physically to create a pure experience for ourselves. Maintain cleanliness of mind and body. It is written in The Ivory Tablets of the Crow:

"Know that when thou have fixed the mind towards the mystical journey of dreams, you must heed the practices of purity. Otherwise, you will face the demons in dreams and have little power over the Gate of Life."

Maintaining purity secures mental focus. When you see those who are easily given over to trends and sloppy homes, pray for them. It is by the divine right of prayer that they may be inspired to leave the gods of depression from which uncleanliness originates.

The power of the Armor of Amaterasu Ohkami is in healing and in the purity of the body and mind. And the Armor of Amaterasu Ohkami contains the same properties as the element jade. It is so that even the uninitiated are attracted to those who wear the Armor. Remember to invoke the Armor three times before and after one has worked with the Ghost Element.

There is another aspect of purity that is known to many Sages, but rarely discussed in the writings preceding this one. Remember the Power of Forgiveness!

The Power of Forgiveness is stronger than many things that are called divine, even gods and goddesses. Forgiveness means that one is free from restraint, free from compulsion, or the mechanical reactions of resentful enslavement.

It is only proper that the Ninzuwu make a rite of forgiveness and apply it within their study and work. When we are reminded of those who have erred against us, we must not give way to resentment. We must remember that resentment is a state of impurity. During times such as these, speak to that memory by saying:

Wohpe Bnhu-Tuu Milda Phe-Tuu-Zhee toci xian
(woh-pay whoo-nn-bee-oot mill-da eh-ph-oot-eehzz toh-she she-an)
Peace be unto you in Memory!

Repeat this phrase sincerely when resentment tries to take hold of the mind. If the ashes of thought still seek to continue their existence, bring the matter up once again after Opening the Celestial Gate in the following words:

The Sacred Text of Ghost Dragon Kotodama

Aum-Tuu-Tuu-Phe vh _____ *Phe-Tuu-Zhee gih -*
Aum-Tuu-Tuu-Phe-Bnhu tala Aum-Hmu-Tuu
(moo-ah-oot-oot-eh-ph vuh _____ *eh-ph-oot-eehzz gee-eh*
moo-ah-oot-oot-eh-ph-whoo-nn-bee tha-la moo-ah-you-
mmh-ha-oot moo-ah-oot-oot-eh-ph-whoo-nn-bee)
I forgive _____ *You are free and I am Free!*

The Rites of Forgiveness are abundant. You will discover
these things when the spirits takes its seat upon the Throne.

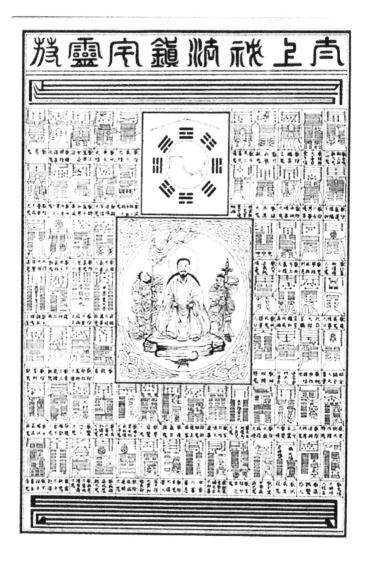

The Taijou Shinsen Chintaku Reifu
太上神仙鎮宅霊符

72 Mirrors of the Bride of Nyarzir

The following text is known in the societies of man as the Taijou Shinsen Chintaku Reifu 太上神仙鎮宅霊符 *and also Tai Shang Lao Jun Zhen Zhai Qi Shi Er Ling Fu* 太上老君镇宅七十二灵符. *And it has been used by the mankind to protect against misfortunes of various types. However, in the Art of Ninzuwu such rites are observed differently. For these are The Books of the Bride of Nyarzir,* 𐤓𐤊𐤎 𐤓𐤋𐤘𐤏 𐤔𐤋𐤈𐤎 𐤓𐤊𐤎 𐤅𐤘𐤓 𐤔𐤋𐤈𐤎 𐤓𐤔𐤋𐤘𐤎𐤏𐤈𐤎 *Uli Qaz Yhi Uli Xau Yhi Nyarzir (you-lee qwaz yeh-hee you-lee shey-aw yeh-hee nigh ar-zeer), and are read to see into the world where the unseen stars reside. Know that the Bride of Nyarzir provide such knowledge that the Earthy Ninzuwu may feed and acquire the use of the Ghost Element. Her words are written in the emotion of thought beyond time:*

"Remembering is what separates Nyarzir from Heaven, and that Nyarzir is Heaven. However, it is not the Heaven of the mortals. Remember, that there have been legends of nations that have boasted of their greatness in the world, but such greatness has come by the extortion and suffering of other nations. It is for this reason that a Netherworld must be present in order for the mortals to have a Heaven, a seemingly beautiful dimension that has acquired such fame by its conquest of certain invisible regions. This is the Heaven of which the mortals ignorantly speak. Nyarzir is not this Heaven.

Nyarzir is the space between the breath and the stillness that exists between change. It is beautiful as it feels and exists as such because of the quality of its being. Let the Ninzuwu of this realm enter our presence that we may be able to study with them directly! Let them participate in the Great Work!

We are Ninzuwu and we have shared our knowledge in stages to both mankind and the Ninzuwu of the seen world. Bestow upon them the Talismans for the Spirit Immortals."

Now thy place of working must be clean with a sweet-smelling incense and salt water sprinkled around thee. Facing the North, you must clap three times and three times must the name Johuta be said. And the Opening of the Sea must occur. And the Soul of Fire Prayer must be performed. The Sword of Ninzuwu must be invoked. After these things have occurred, recite the Baptism of the Ancient One. This is called ꧁꧂ *Uli Vjoh-Aum Aqo (you-lee veh-jo-moo-ah ah-ko), The Jade Palace.*

Once the jade Palace has been established, the Ninzuwu must stare into the Signs of the Places only known to the Magicians of the Secret Lands. And when the Ninzuwu stares into the Signs given herein, they must chant the Name of the Sign, which is its mantra. The length of such an operation is undetermined, save that the mantra and its sign must at least be brought from Zhee to Shki and then from Shki to Zhee. It is known, however, that some Ninzuwu spend hours in such operations, as it develops one's mystical sight and purity.

After the Ninzuwu has developed a relationship with the Living Books of the Bride of Nyarzir, they can entreat such as a form of counsel, as it is written:

"Every day the fiery ones labored and toiled using only their eyes and thoughts as tools. Every night the Goddesses nurtured the scorpionic-architecture of these monuments and temples in their dreams. The Waters were One. Every pleasure in life was found in life itself, and the fiery ones saw that everything was good."

When the operation is finished, call the name Johuta three times, followed by three claps. Here are the signs:

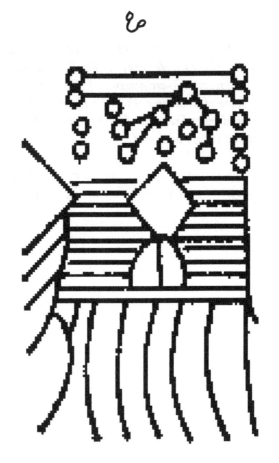

Nasharahisowaka

(nah-sha-rah-hee-so-wa-kah)

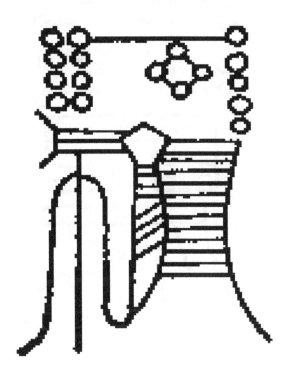

Juwohesamisowaka

(jewh-woh-hay-sah-mee-so-wa-kah)

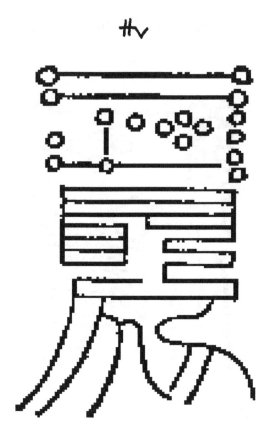

Metohfujisowaka

(may-toh-foo-jee-so-wa-kah)

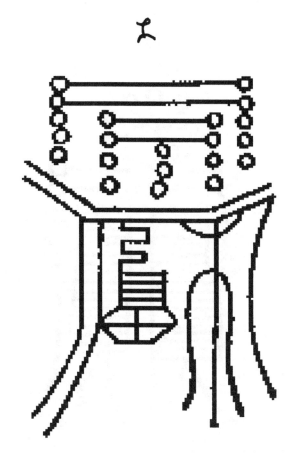

Zabohtufahbisowaka

(zah-bow-too-fah-bee-so-wa-kah)

Azaiwohshamisowaka

(ah-zah-ee-who-shah-mee-so-wa-kah)

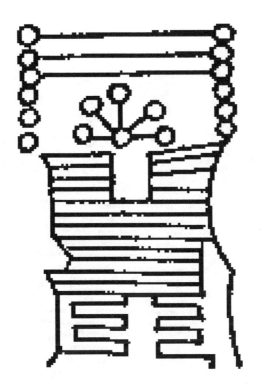

Tohfazumebisowaka

(toh-fah-zoo-may-bee-so-wa-kah)

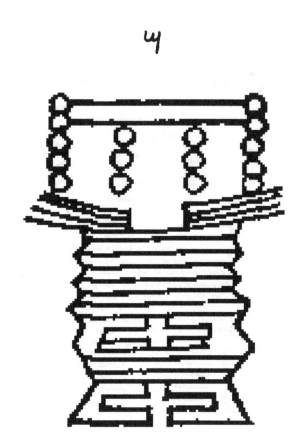

Iohsuremifazohsowaka

(ee-oh-soo-ray-mee-fah-zoh-so-wa-kah)

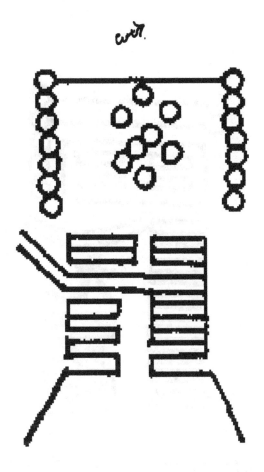

Sahbihatohmezolusowaka

(sah-bee-ha-toh-may-zoh-loo-so-wa-kah)

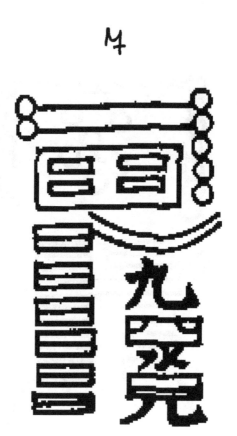

Gamezitubejohrisowaka

(Gah-may-zee-too-bay-joh-ree-so-wa-kah)

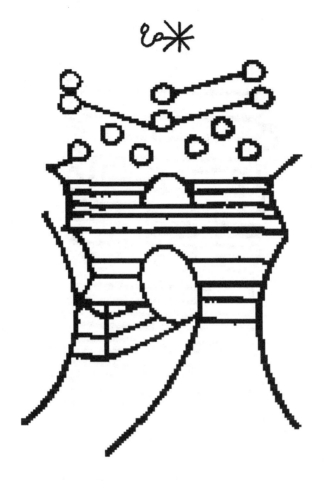

Wahtuxihulohsowaka

(wah-too-she-whoo-loh-so-wa-kah)

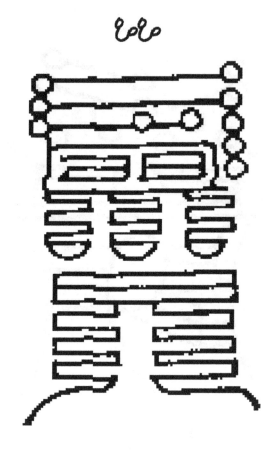

Qwabifohmutihasowaka

(qwah-bee-foh-moo-tee-ha-so-wa-kah)

Yohziahbohwuohkasowaka

(yo-zee-ah-boh-woo-no-kah-so-wa-kah)

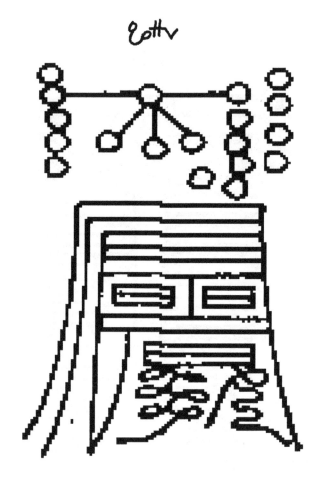

Musohzurefijanosowaka

(moo-soh-zoo-ray-fee-jah-no-so-wa-kah)

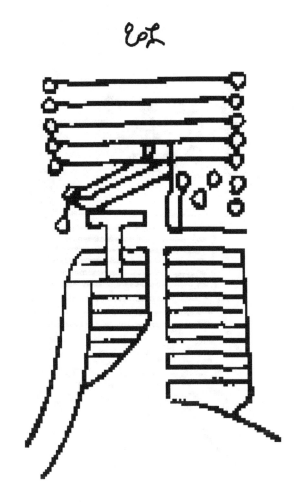

Zuwohkedohbesusowaka

(zoo-who-kay-doe-bay-soo-so-wa-kah)

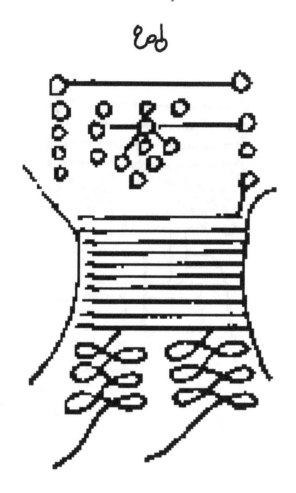

Lohkaxiohmelusowaka

(loh-kah-she-oh-may-loo-so-wa-kah)

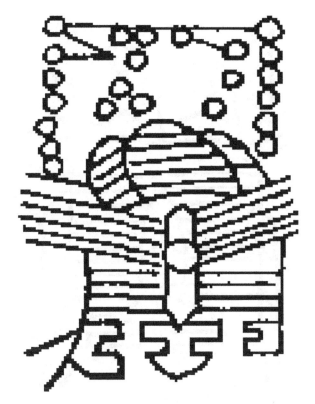

Difusohlimesahzusowaka

(dee-foo-so-whoo-may-sa-zoo-so-wa-kah)

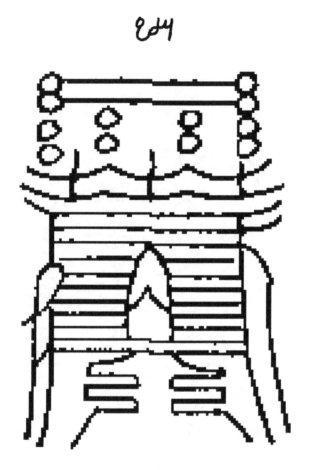

Izunohjakutemisowaka

(ee-zoo-no-jah-koo-tay-mee-so-wa-kah)

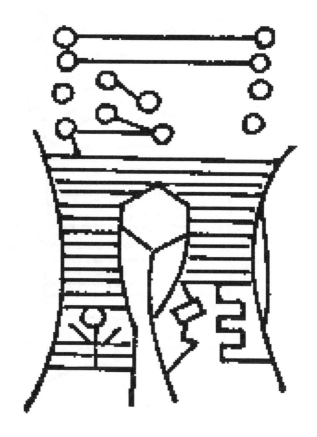

Yiohfasetusasowaka

(yee-no-fah-say-too-sah-so-wa-kah)

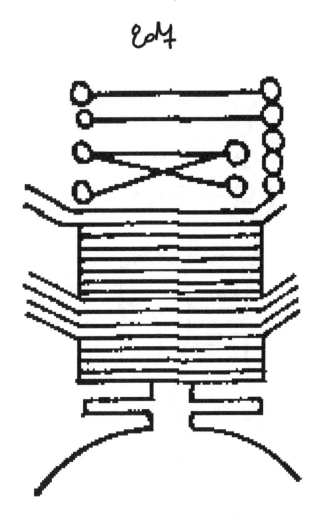

Lihabimusejifohbesowaka

(lee-ha-bee-moo-say-jee-foh-bay-so-wa-kah)

Zusomifaohsewusowaka

(zoo-soh-mee-fah-oh-say-woo-so-wa-kah)

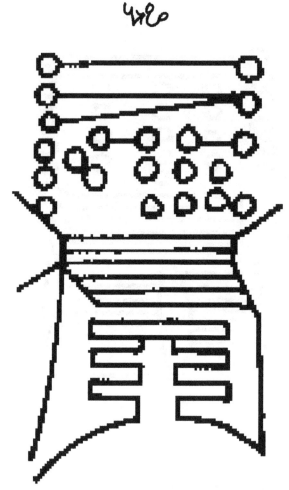

Sefukonohvehusowaka

(say-foo-koh-no-vay-whoo-so-wa-kah)

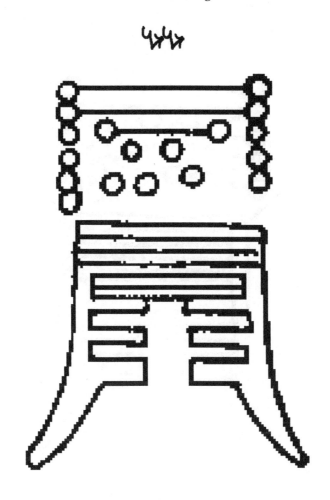

Payuxidanohlutesowaka

(pah-you-she-da-no-loo-tay-so-wa-kah)

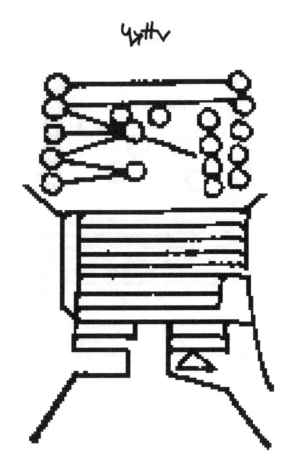

Xiwanufokisefohsowaka

(she-wa-nu-foh-ķee-say-foh-so-wa-ķah)

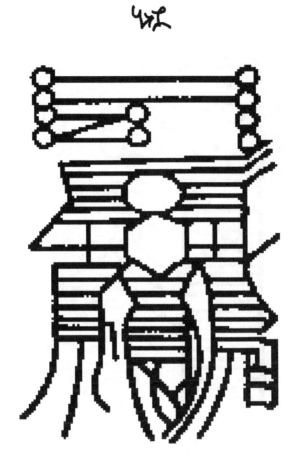

Lepohwasinohsesowaka

(lay-poh-wa-see-no-say-so-wa-kah)

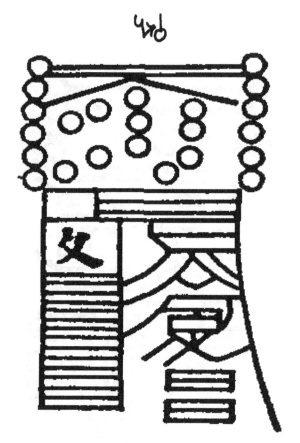

Uzohnibutewalusowaka

(ew-zoh-ee-boo-tay-wa-loo-so-wa-kah)

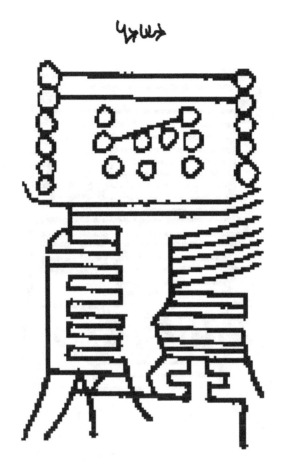

Rojihakenohmisusowaka

(row-jee-ha-kay-no-mi-soo-so-wa-kah)

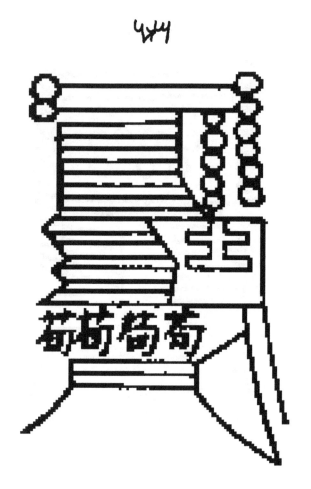

Tohasahinohfuisowaka

(toe-ha-sa-hee-no-foo-ee-so-wa-kah)

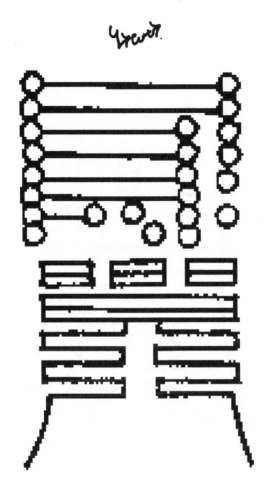

Muyuxinohfalesowaka

(moo-you-she-no-fa-lay-so-wa-kah)

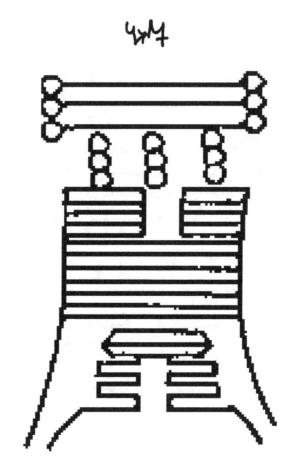

Azinohhasuyiohsowaka

(ah-zee-no-ha-soo-yee-oh-so-wa-kah)

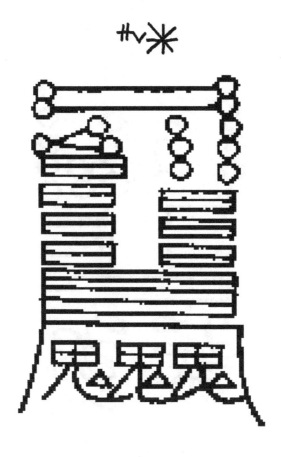

Yewohlibafulumisowaka

(yeh-who-lee-ba-foo-loo-mee-so-wa-kah)

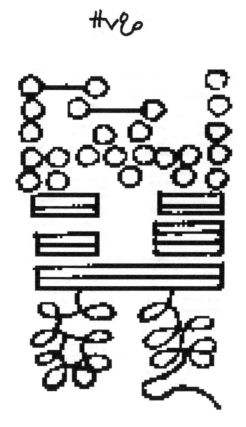

Nohkuxihejohfayusowaka

(no-koo-she-hay-jo-fa-you-so-wa-kah)

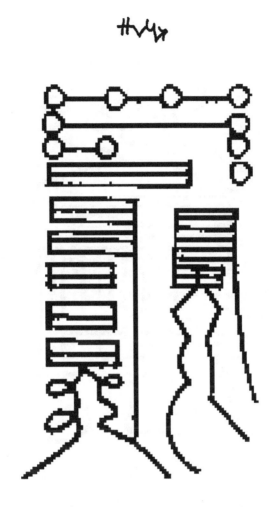

Ujohmidafusohrusowaka

(you-jo-mee-da-foo-so-rue-so-wa-kah)

Wunohsiyedihazusowaka

(woo-no-see-yeh-dee-ha-zoo-so-wa-kah)

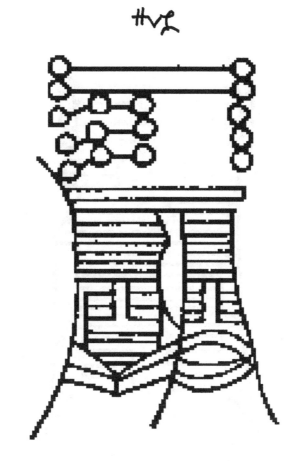

Eloxutohnilewisowaka

(eh-low-shu-toh-nee-lay-wee-so-wa-kah)

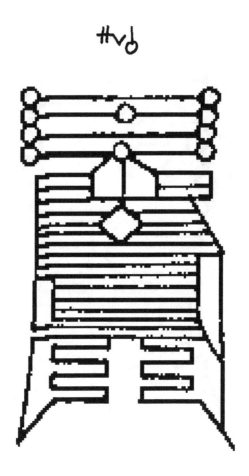

Kifayihuwatenohsowaka

(kee-fa-yee-whoo-wa-tay-no-so-wa-kah)

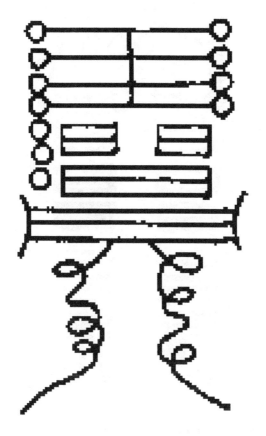

Nuizohawtesohisowaka

(new-ee-zoh-awe-tay-so-ee-so-wa-kah)

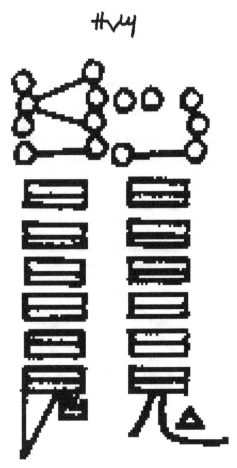

Yikohjasufovasowaka

(yee-koh-ja-sue-foh-vah-so-wa-kah)

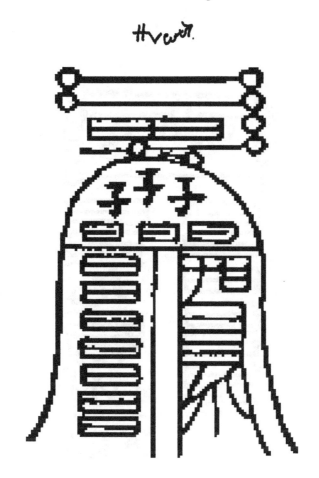

(Oluzidanohwisowaka

(oh-loo-zee-da-noh-wee-so-wa-kah)

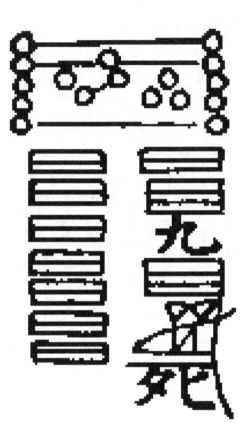

Kofukunohfesowaka

(koh-foo-koo-no-fay-so-wa-kah)

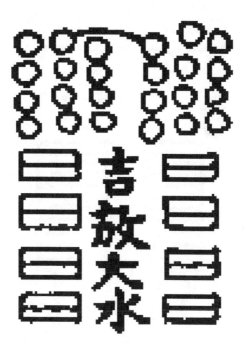

Zanitusewakuhisowaka

(za-nee-too-say-wa-koo-hee-so-wa-kah)

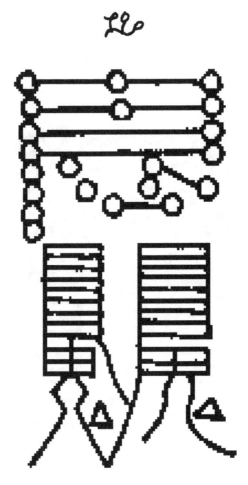

Oxibetunohrisowaka

(oh-she-bay-too-no-ree-so-wa-ka)

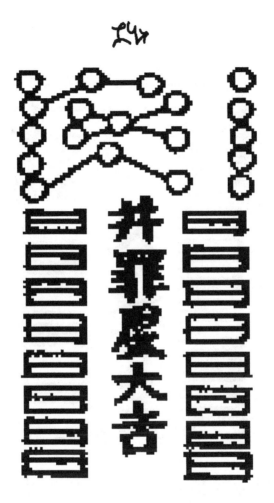

Saduvonihufasowaka

(sa-doo-voh-nee-whoo-fa-so-wa-kah)

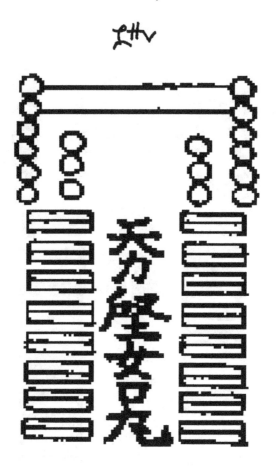

Faziyukedocinusowaka

(fa-zee-you-kay-doh-see-new-so-wa-kah)

Kufabinohaqwasowaka

(koo-fa-bee-no-ha-ahk-wa-so-wa-kah)

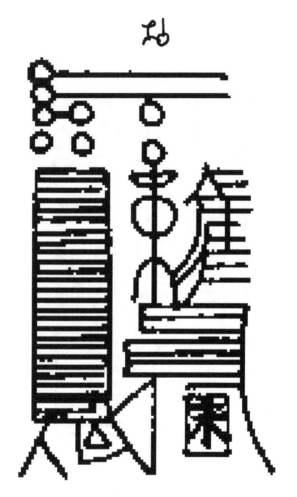

Nujohsaviwabusowaka

(new-jo-sa-vee-wa-boo-so-wa-kah)

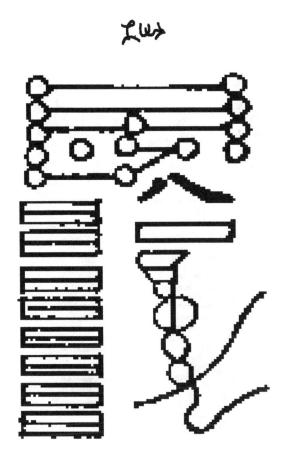

Zugohxitahukosowaka

(zoo-go-she-ta-whoo-koh-so-wa-kah)

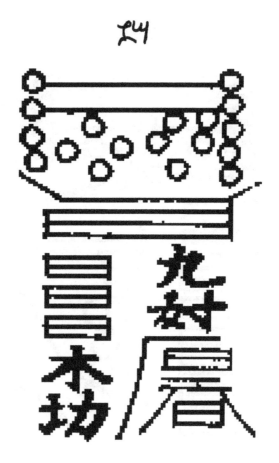

Wuneziludejasowaka

(woo-nay-zee-loo-day-jah-so-wa-kah)

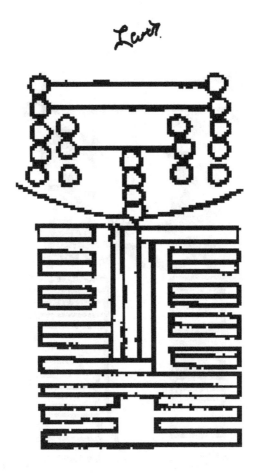

Joxufohmusasowaka

(jo-shu-foh-moo-sa-so-wa-kah)

Hasuyikozinohsowaka

(ha-sue-yee-koh-zee-no-so-wa-kah)

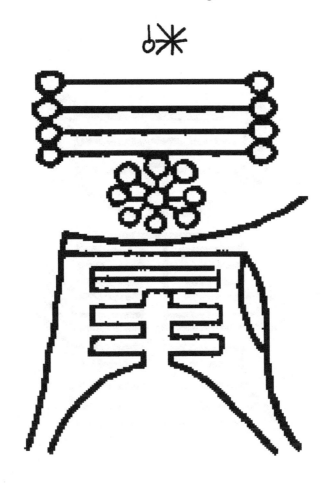

Sujikefoyuvajusowaka

(sue-jee-kay-foh-you-vah-juh-so-wa-kah)

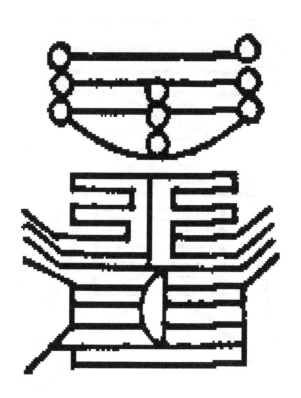

Xodufatiburilusowaka

(sho-doo-fa-tee-boo-ree-loo-so-wa-kah)

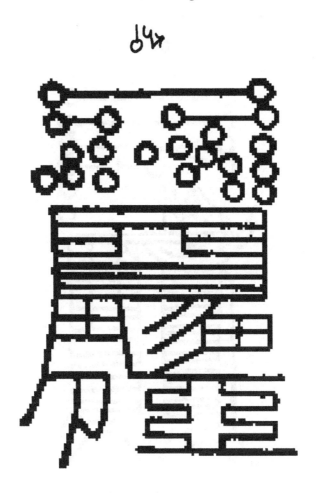

Yikazajohefunohsowaka

(yee-ka-za-jo-hay-foo-no-so-wa-kah)

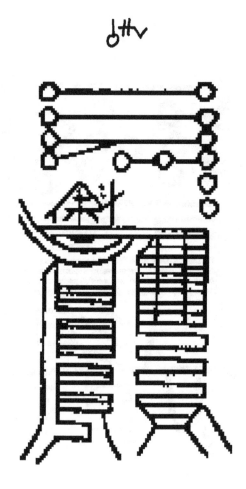

Ikutefaviwohkaesowaka

(ee-koo-tay-fa-vee-who-ka-ee-so-wa-kah)

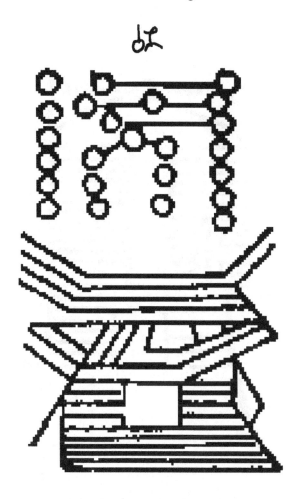

Jubasokiganiyulohsowaka

(juhw-ba-so-kee-ga-nee-you-lo-so-wa-kah)

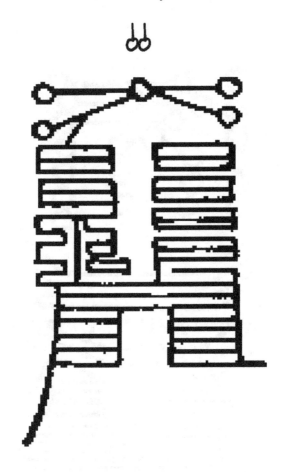

Kawazinohfujitesowaka

(ka-wa-zee-no-foo-jee-tay-so-wa-kah)

Alaxomujobinohsowaka

(ah-la-sho-moo-jo-bee-no-so-wa-kah)

141

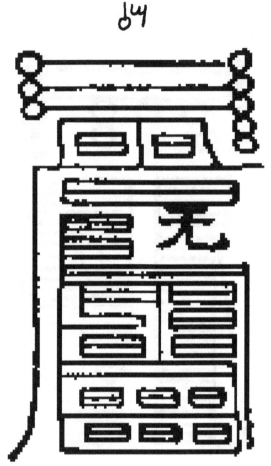

Hozinohjakutufisowaka

(ho-zee-no-ja-koo-too-fee-so-wa-kah)

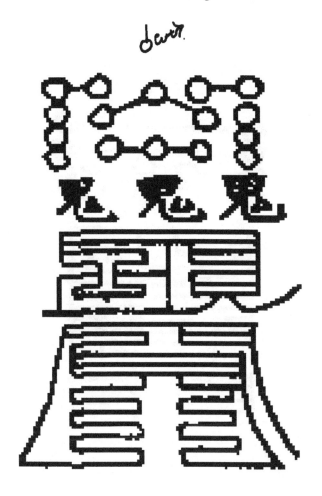

Sigufatisohdazusowaka

(see-goo-fa-tee-so-da-zoo-so-wa-kah)

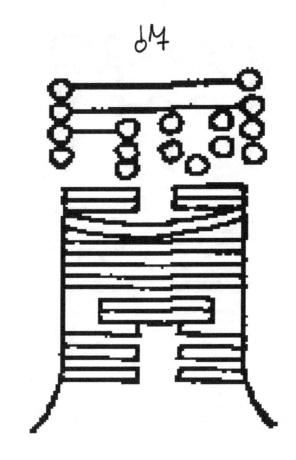

Johbuxiwadakuzisowaka

(jo-boo-she-wa-da-koo-zee-so-wa-kah)

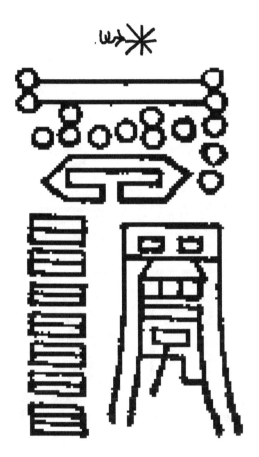

Wuzikufaluhunidosowaka

(woo-zee-koo-fa-loo-whoo-nee-doe-so-wa-kah)

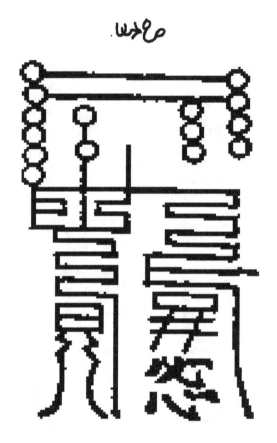

Zunohbeturiseisowaka

(zoo-no-bay-too-ree-say-ee-so-wa-kah)

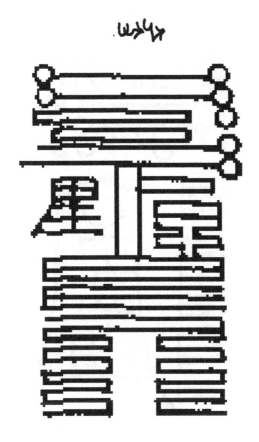

Ikudafiolewnohsasowaka

(ee-koo-da-fi-ole-ooh-no-sa-so-wa-kah)

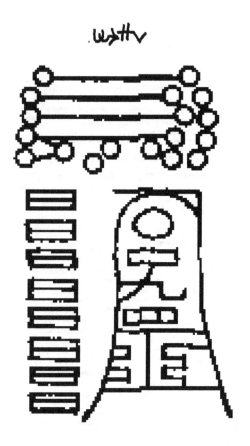

Gudinohsewalusowaka

(goo-dee-no-say-wa-loo-so-wa-kah)

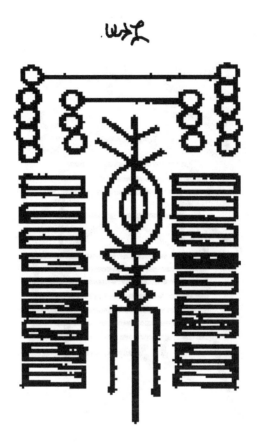

Awerojavokudesowaka

(ah-way-row-ja-voh-koo-day-so-wa-kah)

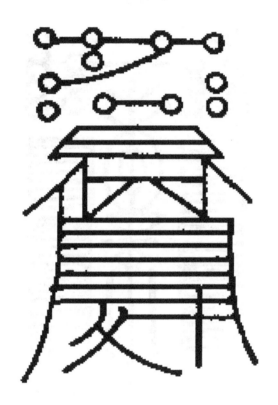

Owozugafunohsowaka

(oh-wo-zoo-ga-foo-no-so-wa-kah)

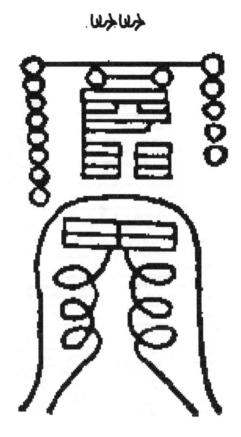

Nuyesiwohabedisowaka

(new-yeh-see-woh-ha-bay-dee-so-wa-kah)

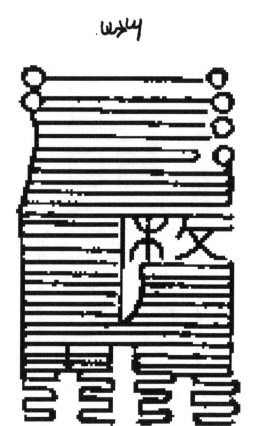

Ewozahunifosowaka

(ee-who-za-whoo-nee-foh-so-wa-kah)

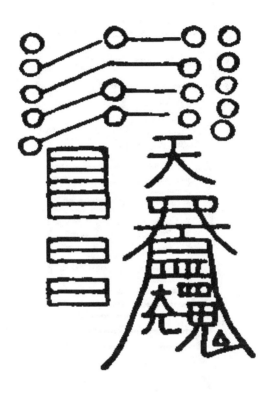

Xuyobidawafusowaka

(shu-yoh-bee-da-wa-foo-so-wa-kah)

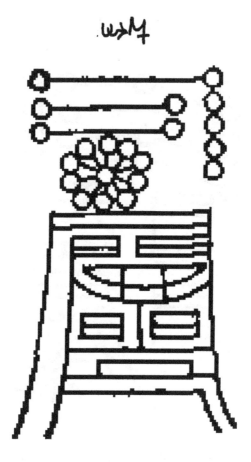

Zisolumihoseisowaka

(zee-so-loo-mee-ho-say-ee-so-wa-kah)

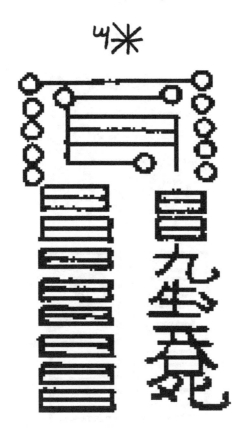

Jikuyohbewanusowaka

(jee-koo-yoh-bay-wa-new-so-wa-kah)

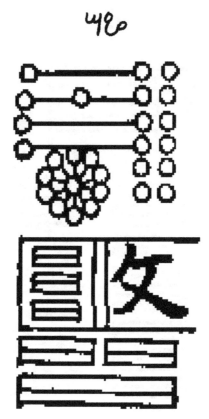

Ixufozatikuyupasowaka

(ee-shu-foh-zateekoo-you-pa-so-wa-kah)

Xowulobafadenohsowaka

(sho-woo-low-ba-fa-day-no-so-wa-kah)

The Book of Ceremonies

Are not the Workers of the Divine World blessed? There is much freedom in the Art of Ninzuwu, as freedom can only be found in the work itself. The Way is One, just as the Waters are One. It is in their foolishness that many have drawn Wandering Spirits to themselves. Indeed some of the greatest civilizations found in the Societies of Man did possess a unique wisdom. This wisdom, however, also created an infatuation with the World of the Dead, and many are deceived by such things.

There is an aspect of the Netherworld that is pure. Its purity is more abundant than that of Heaven. Remember that within the Netherworld exists a Heaven, a Land of the Living, and a World of the Dead. Within the Land of the Living also exists a Heaven, a Land of the Living, and a Netherworld. And so it is in Heaven that we do find the existence of a Heaven, a Land of the Living, and a Netherworld. These things are written about previously, but again are stated for the sake of purity.

Many will try to use a lie as a truth and a truth as a lie. Turn away from these things. Stay vigilant and remember not to get swayed by the thinking of the nations. This work is a special work with a purpose all to its own. Let the profane have their way. Although some of their rites may appear to be similar to our own, these are not to be confused with the rites sacred to the Art of Ninzuwu. Perhaps, it can even be said that some of these things are useful to some, but still they are to be avoided. Once Ninzuwu has been cultivated at a glimpse, it can only be nurtured with its own. Other things may not be harmful in itself, but the energies will not merge with that of our own. It is for this reason that many will not pray at two different shrines even though each hold a kami.

When you see a man cry out in a state of ecstasy claiming that he wants to heal people, know that this person is a victim of Wandering Spirits. In this newfound desire to heal people, this same man will then seek to learn some occult teaching that will only nurture his being possessed by wicked spirits.

After he has learned some occult techniques on how to heal people and has ignorantly strengthened his ties with these very same demons, misfortunes will begin to happen with those who are closely-related. These misfortunes are caused by the same demons that put the idea in his head of wanting to heal people. It is unfortunate that so many people fall prey to this design that the Wandering Spirits has created.

In order to enter the work of healing, a person must first work on themselves. They must understand that the world is always the result of the thoughts that linger in the minds of the masses. If a person feels that they are here to heal the world, it is only because of their negative perception of it. If one is to truly heal the world, then they must change the thinking of the masses of the world. If the world is negative, it is because of the negative thoughts that are being produced by the majority of those living in the world. Therefore, if a person is to change the world, they must change the way people think. They must have knowledge of certain invisible laws, and how the violation of these can *damage the mind and body. These things are not found in an occult technique, but in the study of our very own being.*

During the Eternal Path of Renewal, situations may arise where we meet those who are in distress and in ill-health. Heal freely. Healing is a part of the work, but is not the work itself. Heal freely. Remember to always keep this work pure. Think not of the techniques, but of the development of one's character. Are we still poor in spirit that we are to think negatively of those who have offended us? Surely, we have much work to do on ourselves and in such work is the true meaning of the magical arts. How can we maintain our health spiritually while digesting the impure emotions of anger and resentment? Many are lost.

Our work in these ceremonial rites, contained herein, is for the advancement of an otherworldly consciousness by shedding negative emotions. It is by way of these ceremonies that we learn the customs of an invisible fraternal order, from which we descend. Nothing is without order or exists just for the sake of existence, as the hexarchy of our ancestry extends into the unseen regions. Still this world is in a sort of prehistoric stage of development, the crest that will lead to a very advanced technology that is found in nature.

ᛕᛕᛉ ᚠᛉᛉ ᚼᛁᚳᛠᛉ ᛕᛕᛉ ᚤᚳᛁᚲᚤᛉᛠᛠᛂᛉ

Always remember the Chant of the Ayaqox. It is a unique rite that has been preserved from a timeless space for those who live in the shadow. These too will rise in Dreams. Prepare thy space for working in the North. It is the Rite of the Full Moon. Remember, to pay respect and tribute for we are allowed to venture forth.

Now the altar is one made the burning of pine incense. Two white candles should be lit and the Stone Bowl of Eternity also present with salt water sprinkled around the chamber. Clap three times and call the name Johuta three times.

Perform the Opening of the Sea. Recite the Soul of Fire Prayer three times. Pray. Call the Shamuzi. Invoke the Sword of Ninzuwu. Afterwards, prepare a fire in the Stone Bowl of Eternity and call Wutzki. Once the fire has been prepared, you must recite this incantation:

Ayaqox Sharra-itu Hmu-Phe-Phe-Nzu
(I-yah-qaus shar-rah-ee-too you-mmh-ha-eh-ph-eh-ph-ooh-zz-nn)
Ayaqox prosperity bring forth!

Ayaqox Hmu-Phe-Phe-Nzu lil.
(I-yah-quas *you-mmh-ha-eh-ph-eh-ph-ooh-zz-nn lel*)
Ayaqox, bring forth understanding!

Toci ny Aum-Zhee-Bnhu Bnhu-Phe-Tuu mafdet
(toh-she nigh moo-ah-eehzz-whoo-nn-bee whoo-nn-bee-eh-ph-oot maff-deht)
In divine love we walk!

Sol Ayaqox uli shintai yhi su
(sole I-yah-uas you-lee sh-in-tie yeh-hee soo)
Remember Ayaqox the passion of awareness!

Aum-Aum-Phe-Hmu Ayaqox uli ryu
(moo-ah-moo-ah-eh-ph-you-mmh-ha I-yah-quas you-lee rlee-you)
Protect Ayaqox, thy dreams!

And you are to repeat this incantation once for every space, from Zhee to Shki and from Shki to Zhee. And when this rite is performed, many wondrous things will take place, even in thy sight. After the Ninzuwu has completed thy cycle of this incantation, thee must clap they hands three times after repeating the name Johuta three times.

Witnesses of the Resurrection

And it must be remembered that the 72 Books of the Bride of Nyarzir, the Ghost Maiden, should not be used as a form of divination other than what is instructed earlier. Below are the 72 witnesses who provide ample testimony to the Ghost Maiden that the Seven Dragon have been resurrected.

Know that these Witnesses are the result of the Seven Ghost Dragon having each passed through the Nine Books of the Vasuh language. There are Nine Witnesses for each of the Seven Ghost Dragons. And in thy work in acquiring virtue, you will surely see them come to life.

ℰ家族の紛争を解決し、より良い環境を作ります。 *Settling family disputes and making better environment.*

Ѱ富、仕事、と繁栄を増加させます。 *Increases wealth, work, and prosperity.*

♯∨社会の中で3.増加の状態 *Increase status in society.*

人負の人々を避けるため、財産を保護します。 *Protect property, avoid negative people.*

家の真ん中を支配地球神を落ち着かせ。床の上や地面に家の中心にお守りを配置します。
Calms Earth God who rules middle of the house. Place amulet in center of the house on floor or in the ground.

犯罪や詐欺的な人々を避けてください。
Avoid crime and fraudulent people.

悪霊や病気を作成しているものをはじきます。
Repels evil spirits and those that create sickness.

.成功と繁栄を作成するのに役立ちます.
Success and helps create prosperity.

悪魔から呪いを防ぎます。 *Prevents curses from demons.*

刑事ビジネス慣行を防止します。 *Prevents criminal business practices.*

法廷で良好な転帰を促進します。
Promotes good outcome in court.

ᘒ病気を撃退し、治癒を促進します。 *Repels sickness and promotes healing.*

ᘒコミュニティで他の人と成功を作成するのに役立ちます。 *Helps creates success in community and with others.*

ᘒ家に入るの負の動物霊と悪霊のを防ぎます。 *Prevents negative animal spirits and evil spirits from entering the house.*

ᘒ事故や家族の呪いを防ぎます。 *Prevents accidents and family curses.*

ᘒ良い食品、健康的な水を食べて推進しています。 *Promotes eating good foods, healthy water.*

ᘒ心臓発作、突然死を防止します。健康を促進します。 *Prevents heart attacks, sudden death. Promotes good health.*

病気の動物を癒します。負のアニマル・スピリットを追放するための良いです。 *Heal sick animals. Good for banishing negative animal spirits.*

幽霊を払拭します。 *Dispels hauntings.*

負のエンティティと悪意に満ちた精神的な読者に起因する被害を防止します。 *Prevents harm caused by negative entities and spiteful psychic readers.*

防ぎはテロ、戦争、暴徒の暴力の被害者であること。 *Prevents being a victim of terrorism, war, mob violence.*

悪い予言夢を受信した後、良好な運命を作成します。 *Creates good fate after receiving a bad prophetic dream.*

病気、悪天候によって引き起こされる、特に病気を防ぎます。 *Prevents illness, especially sicknesses caused by bad weather.*

收穫を増加させます。投資から戻ります。
Increases harvest. Return from investments.

干ばつを緩和します。ドラゴン神を静めます。
Relieves drought. Calms dragon deity.

精神的な攻撃の中、心の穏やかなを保持
します。 *Keeps mind calm during spiritual attack.*

家庭で盗難や障害を防ぎます。 *Prevents theft and disturbances in home.*

家の東の神を落ち着かせます。家の東に入
れてください。 *To calm deity of the east of the house. Put in the east of house.*

家の西の神を落ち着かせます。家の西に置
きます。 *To calm deity of the west of the house. Put in the west of house.*

損失アイテムを回復します。家の北の乱れ
を抑制するために北朝鮮に置いてください。
Recover loss items. Place in North to curb disturbances in North of home.

〷Ⴒこの領域に配置されたときに31は、家の南の乱れを防止します。*Prevents disturbances in South of the house when placed in this area.*

〷成功と幸運を促進します。 *Promotes success and good fortune.*

〷癒す病気や悪霊を離れて変わります。*Heals sickness and turns away demons.*

〷家庭での現象を引き起こす精神を削除します。 *Removes spirits that cause phenomena in home.*

〷異常気象の後に悪い運命を抑止します。*Deters ill-fate after unusual weather.*

〷事故や早期死亡を防止します。 *Prevents accidents and premature death.*

〷犯罪者や家族の不幸をはじきます。豊かな子孫を促進します。 *Repels criminals and family misfortunes. Promotes prosperous offspring.*

卄∨ᗯ刈負の霊による妨害をはじきます。 *Repels disturbances by negative spirits.*

卄∨Ꮇ治療法は、材料アイテムの損失の上に心配します。 *Cures worry over loss of material items.*

⽊米癒す疾患。 *Heals disease.*

⽊Ɛⵜ成功を妨害する悪霊を追放します。 *Banishes evil spirits that interfere with success.*

⽊Ꮴ安全な旅行を促進します。盗難を抑止します。 *Promotes safe travel. Deters theft.*

⽊卄∨自然災害から43保護。病気や病気を防ぐことができます。*Protection from natural disasters. Prevents disease and sickness.*

⽊⽊心、疲労感、そして狂気を癒します。 *Heals the mind, tiredness, and insanity.*

悪霊、それらによる影響の礼拝を阻止します
Deters worship of evil spirits and the effects caused by them.

出産前後の悪はじきます。 *Repels evil before and after childbirth.*

悪削除します。 *Removes evil.*

家畜やペットの死の後の家族の呪いを防ぎます。 *Prevents curse of family members after the death of livestock and pets.*

同じ地区や家庭で再発死亡や事故の量を減らすために使用します。このような環境に住んでいる家族を保護します。 *Used to reduce the amount of recurrent deaths and accidents in the same neighborhood or home. Protects family living in such environments.*

ペット、浮遊動物、そして非常識な家畜から損傷を防ぎます。 *Prevents injury from pets, stray animals, and insane livestock.*

幸せな家庭生活を促進します。家族の不幸を防ぐことができます。 *Promotes happy family life. Prevents family misfortune.*

幽霊を防止します。 *Prevents hauntings.*

心を落ち着かせると悪防ぐことができます。 *Calming the heart and prevents evil.*

邪悪な恒星の運命と邪悪な魔術師に対して54シールズ。*Shields against evil stellar fates and wicked magicians.*

動揺神による55防ぎファミリー病気や病気。*Prevents family illness and sickness due to upset deity.*

幻覚と悪夢を防ぎます。 *Prevents hallucinations and nightmares.*

健康な家畜を促進します。動物を癒します。 *Promotes healthy livestock. Heals animals.*

不安やストレスを軽減します。 *Reduces anxiety and stress.*

悪霊によって行われた攻撃をはじきます。
Repels attacks made by evil spirits.

保護。安全な旅行やビジネスを保証します。 *Protection against theft. Insures safe travel and business.*

作物を保護します。 *Protect crops.*

病気を防ぎ、健康を復元します。 *Prevents disease and restores health.*

のろいスピリッツ、不幸をはじきます。
Repels cursing spirits and misfortunes.

災害をはじきます。守護霊を強化します。
Repels disaster. Strengthens guardian spirits.

ﱤは死者と放浪霊の負の霊をはじきます。

Repels negative spirits of the dead and wandering spirits.

ﱤﱤは、メモリを復元します。治癒する疾患。

Restores memory. Heals disease.

ﱤは、家庭の平和を促進します。積極的な動物からの農民を保護します。 *Promotes peace in household. Protects farmer from aggressive animals.*

悪の霊をはじきます。成功を増加させます。 *Repels evils spirits. Increases success.*

は、ビジネスやご家族での平和的な関係を促進します。 *Promotes peaceful relationships in business and family.*

ビジネスがよりよくできるようにします。成功。

Makes business better. Success.

がんばろうを促進します。 *Promotes good luck.*

ЦЦѪは害を防止します。平和な家庭を推進してい
ます *Prevents harm. Promotes peaceful household.*

Immortal Rites of the Ancestors

*Know that the gods and goddesses of legend, and in the
histories of mankind, exist in the Heaven of the
Netherworld and no higher. The human race is still in its
prehistoric stage. If there is any evolution, then it is in
acquiring new emotions. How can humanity not exist in its
prehistoric stage, if the only emotions they know are often*

expressed by animals? Our work, the true magic, is not found in ritual, but in working on ourselves, in acquiring higher emotions that nourish the spirit.

We descend from a space that is beyond the stars, an etheric platform that knows not death. This is where the science of the ghost element originates. It is a sexual realm and was studied by those who constructed Tachikawa-ryu 立川流. These things will become clearer when the rites contained in this text are exercised. However, the work of virtue must remain prominent before all else. Work on Thyself.

Keep thy heart and mind pure. When the sacred work of the Ghost Dragons has begun, thy perception shall increase greatly and the true nature of the universe will be seen more easily. Know too, that while some of the energies listed in this text are used by the wise nations, they do not have the formula to call the greatest potential of these things.

Since there is nothing to worship, pray to your ancestors. Honor your ancestors in order to strengthen humanity. The race of humanity is by nature the ruler of the seen universe, but it so happened that the gods of the Heaven of the Netherworld feed off of this same race. And the human race became enslaved and cutoff from their true heritage. Do not be afraid of these things as they must happen. It is the same way with a child, who in infancy can only discern its parents' presence by sound and scent. However, when the child reaches a certain age, it can use its five senses to recognize its parents very easily. So it is the same with the Race of Man. Man is still in a stage of infancy. There are still lessons to be learned. And it must occur that those who are skilled in the Art of Ninzuwu must create a *pantheon of their own ancestors and pray to them for guidance and strength.*

When the time is ready to entreat your ancestors, prepare to enter the Immortal Realm. Build an altar to the North. Attune to the plant, which serves as your shrine. Three claps and recite Johuta three times. And there should be two white candles present. Let the burning of Frankincense and Myrrh also come into being. Sprinkle salt water around thee and begin the Opening of the Sea. Perform the Soul of Fire Prayer three times. Pray. Call the Shamuzi and Invoke the Sword of Ninzuwu.

Once the Temple of the Ninzuwu has been created, you must perform the Amatsu Norito three times. After these are called into being, the Ninzuwu must recite the name of the Heaven Parent, the actual name of the Divine. This name must be recited through the Nine Dreams from Zhee to Shki and from Shki to Zhee in the following manner:

Ame-yudzuru-hi-ame-no-sa-giri-kuni-yudzuru-tsuki-kuni-no-sa-giri-no-Mikoto
Harae-Tamae (cleanse all)
Kiyome-Tamae (purify all)
Mamori-Tamae (protect all)
Sakihae-Tamae (may all beings be happy)

Facing the North, the Ninzuwu must call upon the Black Warrior, Bishamonten:

Bishamonten Mamori-Tamae, Sakihae Tamae (twice)
おん　べいしらまなや　そわか
On Beishiramanaya Sowaka (thrice)

The Sacred Text of Ghost Dragon Kotodama

Facing the East, the Ninzuwu must call upon the
Guardian of the Nation, Jikokuten:

Jikokuten Mamori-Tamae, Sakihae Tamae (twice)
おん　ぢりたらしゅたら
らら　はらまだな　そわか
On Chiritara Shutara
Rara Haramadana Sowaka (thrice)

Facing the South, The Ninzuwu must call upon the One
who Expands, Zochoten:

Zochoten Mamori-Tamae, Sakihae Tamae (twice)
おん　びろだきゃ　やきしゃ
ぢはたえい　そわか
On Birodakya Yakisha Jihataei Sowaka (thrice)

Facing the West, the Ninzuwu must call upon the One
who Sees through Evil, Komokuten:

Komokuten Mamori-Tamae, Sakihae Tamae (twice)
おん　びろばくしゃ　のうぎゃ
ぢはたえい　そわか
On Birobakusha Nōgya Chihataei Sowaka (thrice)

Facing the Sky in thy mind, the Ninzuwu must call the
Lord of Protection, Taishakuten:

Taishakuten Mamori-Tamae, Sakihae Tamae (twice)
おん　しゃきらや　そわか

Warlock Asylum

On Shakiraya Sowaka (thrice)

After the Gatekeepers of the Immortal Realms have been called, One can then entreat their ancestors of the upper realms. And the choice of which ancestors are best suited for the task will come to thee during the initiatory workings. Let it flow like Water.

All Dreams are born out of Water. The subconscious mind releases its wastes through Dreams. This process was written about long ago when Ukemochi-no-Mikoto was slain by Tsukiyomi-no-Mikoto. And Ukemochi-no-Mikoto did spit food from her mouth that was to feed humanity. Disgusting as it may seem, this was, and is, symbolic of the process of the subconscious mind spewing out Dreams from within itself, which are slained by the Lord of the Moon, Tsukiyomi-no-Mikoto.

Based on these things, the Ninzuwu must recognize the Dream for what it is. If the meaning is not known, write it down and do not search any further for it. Only observe the processes in life and let things be as they are. Dreams are teachers of how the subconscious mind creates reality. If Dreams are messages from the gods, as some believe, then it is only the gods of the Heaven of the Netherworld, and this is still the subconscious mind. The Ninzuwu can create these Dreams for themselves by allowing the Spirit to sit upon the Throne. All of these things have been recorded in The Ivory Tablets of the Crow.

During the operations contained in this text, thy garments must be clean, and of either a black or white color. If a uniform that is made specific for these rites can be obtained, though it is not necessary, the garment should have no markings, as it will interfere with the frequency of the Signs you are about to receive. And keep the Sign of the Immortals in the North of the Temple. And this is the Sign of the Immortals:

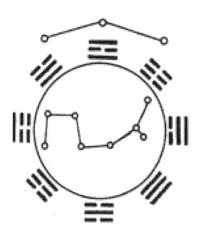

And the only tool that is in the possession of the Ninzuwu is the Sword. And one must get a fine piece of wood or a long crystal and engrave of paint this Sign upon it, as it is to be used in the preceding rites, always in thy right hand. This is the Sign that must be inscribed upon thy tool of working:

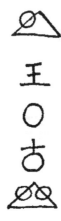

Preserve these few things that must be preserved for the generation of thy own initiation. It is an endless work of many ages.

Amatsu Norito

*Taka ama hari ni Kamu zumari masu Kamurogi Kamuromi
no Mikoto moshite
Sumemi oya Kamu Izanagi no Ohkami Tsukushi no
Himuka no Tachibana no
Odo no Awagigahara ni Misogi harae tamaishi
Toki ne are maseru
Harae do no Ohkami tachi Moromoro no Maga goto
Tsumi kegare-o
Harae tamae Kiyome tamae to Maosu kotono Yoshi-o
Amatsu kami Kunitsu kami Yao yorozu no Kami tachi
tomo ni Kikoshi mese to
Kashi komi Kashi komi mo mao su*

The Ninzuwu Language

0. = ✳ 1. = ℰ 2. = ⅄ 3. = ⧺

4. = ⅃ 5. = ⅄ 6. = ⱳ 7. = ⅄

8. = ⱳ 9. = Ⅿ

A. = Φ B. = Ⱬ C. = Ⅹ D. = ⊦ₒ

E. = ⅀ F. = ✕ G. = Ⅾ H. = ⧦

I. = ⨂ J. = A K. = ⧸ L. = Ⅼ

M. = Ⱬ N. = Ⱬ O. = Ⱳ Q. = Ⅹ

R. = ◎ S. = Ⅰ T. = ⧫ U. = Ⱪ

V. = ☉ W. = Ⱦ X. = Ψ Y. = ⅃ℓ

Z. = ⅌

Invoking the Hexagrams

The Rite of the Hexagram is very simple, and should not be taken lightly. One must prepare the Temple of the Ninzuwu, which is to be place in the North. And the burning of Cedar and Pine incense must be brought into being. White candles are to be lit. Sprinkle salt water around the place of your operations and begin The Opening of the Sea. Perform the Soul of Fire Prayer thrice. Call the Shamuzi and invoke the Sword of Ninzuwu. Recite the Amatsu Norito and call the Heavenly Parent.

After these things have occurred, you must bring the name of the said power along with its mantra, as it appears in The Yi Jing Apocrypha of Genghis Khan, through the Nine Dreams, from Zhee to Shki and from Shki back to Zhee. If the 23rd Hexagram is ruled by Shikiyamatsumi-no-Kami and the Vasuh letters associated with this Hexagram are Phe-Hmu, then the mantra for this Hexagram is Shikiyamatsumi-no-Kami-eh-ph-you-mmh-ha. Once the rite is accomplished and the mantra is invoked, recite Johuta three times and clap three times.

Vasuh Language

Since the publication of The Ivory Tablets of the Crow, much has been revealed about what is known as the Vasuh language. First, we have the set of numbers, which are used to compose words. These numerical letters and grapheme is called an Asaru. The *asaru* are activated by its proper pronunciation, which is reversed to how the numerical letter is written. The esoteric reason for the use of numbers as letters has a lot to do with merging the left and right hemispheres of the brain, the alchemical marriage. Here are a few examples of how this works:

The term *star* as translated from the Vasuh Glossary is *zhee-shki-tuu-phe,* but the pronunciation is in reverse and as follows:

"ehzz-eek-hss-oot-eh-ph"

Thus, we find that the *asaru* are activated by a reverse pronunciation of the written term. While the reader may find it difficult to remember the terms in the Vasuh Glossary, and then have the task of pronouncing each term in reverse, there is a very simple method of employing the language of dreams that every Initiate must remember,-is that the Vasuh language is based on the principles of mathematics.

Many scholars have stated that the terms found in the Vasuh Glossary are terms that were derived from the practice of telepathy, wherein the shaman would repeat a certain phrase while visualizing and individual and were able to alter reality. The process of how these mantras were created had a lot to do with knowing the mathematical sum of a word regardless of the language spoken. For example, the English term god can be said to have the following mathematical sum: g (7) + o (15) + d (4) = 26. This equation would translate to Nzu (7), plus 1 and 5 equals 6, since "o" is the 15th letter of the English alphabet, it is reduced to its lowest sum, which would be Phe (6), plus Hmu (4). Thus the Vasuh term for god would be *nzu-phe-hmu*. It's pronunciation would then be:

"ooh-zz-nn-eh-ph-you-mmh-ha"

An understanding of this term comes through determining the meaning of each asaru, or letter.

Nzu = *"Can be used as a protective shield, or to heal cuts and wounds. "*
Phe = *"It affects the quality of the emotions and useful for the arts of levitation."*
Hmu = *"Increases sexual energy and the eyesight"*

Therefore, the English term god is translated into the Vasuh language as *Nzu-Phe-Hmu* meaning, a protective shield affecting the emotions, increasing sexual energy. However, we can get a more exact meaning by reducing the sum of these asaru to its lowest value, which would be Nzu (7) + Phe (6) + Hmu (4) equals 17. We would then take 17 and reduce it as follows: Zhee (1) + Nzu (7) equal 8.

Therefore, a clear definition of god is equal to 8, or the asaru Lewhu, pronounced *ooh-wel*. The attribute of Lewhu are as follows:

"It is used in initiating one to the divine energies of the stars."

Thus, we find that the definition of "god" is the Initiate who uses the divine energies of the stars. It is important that the Initiate of The Cult of Nyarzir understands the importance of using this formulae to translate mystical incantations.

By use of the *mathematical language of dreams,* the Initiate can also interpret and communicate with the same forces that he/she are being influenced by, and what deity that they may call upon for clarity.

Aside from the alpha-numerical aspects of the Ninzuwu language, there are an additional 27 letters. These are written as they appear and pronounced the same as their English equivalent. This means that the entire alphabet of the Ninzuwu language is made up of 36 letters.

The Ninzuwu language can also be used as a "code" language, or substitute for English, so as to keep certain esoteric writings secret. However, for those who have chosen the Art of Ninzuwu as a path, it is most necessary to learn, both Japanese and the Ninzuwu language. Within the inner teaching of Ninzuwu is a deeper knowledge of how this to employ this language.

φ

A – El (ehl) ✳

Abandon – Dika (dee-kah)

Abandoned – Dika-Shki (dee-kah eek-hss)

Abdomen – Tiki (tee-kee)

Abiding – Shki-Nzu (eek-hss-ooh-zz-nn)

Ability – Hmu-Tuu (you-mmh-ha-oot)

Able – Jeh (jay)

Abomination – Nedu (neh-do)

About – Aum-Shki (moo-ah-eek-hss)

Above – Lewhu-Nzu-Hmu (ooh-wel-ooh-zz-nn-you-mmh-ha)

Above the firmaments - Lewhu-Nzu-Zhee (ooh-wel-ooh-zz-nn-eehzz)

Abundance – Orisha (ore-ree-sha)

Abyss – Kujo (koo-jo)

Accept – Thor (th-ore)

Accuse – Bewh (beh-weh)

Accuser (an accuser) - Bewhiu (beh-weh-ee-you)

Act - Tuu-Shki – (oot-eek-hss)

Action - Zi (zee)

Add - Shki-Bnhu – (eek-hss-who-nn-bee)

After – Warki – (war-key)

Afterwards – Uqa (you-qwa)

Against – Etu (eh-too)

Age, Adept, Ages – Zhee-Aum (eehzz-moo-ah)

Aid – Tak (tahk)

All - Zhee-Shki-Phe-Tuu-Tuu (eehzz-eek-hss-eh-ph-oot-oot)

All creatures - Zhee-Bnhu (eehzz-whoo-nn-bee)

Alliance – Katoh (ka-toe)

Alone – Beli (beh-lee)

Altar – Shamu (sha-moo)

Always - Shki-Aum (eek-hss-moo-ah)

Am (I am) - Aum-Hmu-Tuu (moo-ah-you-mmh-ha-oot)

Am (I am the lord your god) - Aum-Shki-Zhee (moo-ah-eek-hss-eehzz)

Amidst - Nzu-Phe (ooh-zz-nn-eh-ph)

Among - Lewhu-Nzu-Bnhu (ooh-wel-ooh-zz-nn-whoo-nn-bee)

Ancestor/Ancestors – Ninazu (nen-ah-zoo)

And – Tala (tha-la)

Angel - Shki-Zhee-Phe (eek-hss-eehzz-eh-ph)

Angle - Phe-Bnhu (eh-ph-whoo-nn-bee)

Another - Lewhu-Phe (ooh-wel-eh-ph)

Any – Sum (soom)

Anything – Sumsah (soom-sa)

Are – Gih (gee-eh)

Arise - Bnhu-Zhee (whoo-nn-bee-eehzz)

Army – Vehz (veh-zz)

Ark - Shki-Hmu-Aum (eek-hss-you-mmh-ha-moo-ah)

Arrive – Ilusv (ee-luu-sev)

Artisans – Yec (yeck)

As – Ki (kee)

Ashes – Ditalu (dee-tah-luu)

Assembly – Ussi (ooh-ss-ee)

Astral body – Yuki (you-kee)

Astral RealmS – Kunlun (khun-loon)

Attacker – Gudaxa (goo-dach-ah)

Attract – She (shee)

At – Cxu (cach-oo)

Aura – Nin (nen)

Awareness – Su (soo)

Awake – Owoa (oh-wo-ah)

Awaken – Nuwa (new-wah)

Awesome – Kashuri (kah-shure-ee)

Axe - AhTuu (ah-oot)

Aixu – Dragon of Mercury (ay-eye-zoo)

ح

Baby – Vepu (veh-poo)

Back – Seru (seh-rue)

Bad – Leffu (leh-foo)

Barely – Sei (say-ee)

Bat – Camutz (ca-mu-tss)

Battle – Tazu (tah-zoo)

Be – Bnhu-Tuu (whoo-nn-bee-oot)

Bear – Nasi (nah-see)

Become – Hmu-Phe (you-mmh-ha-eh-ph)

Bed – Ershe (ur-shay)

Beer – Sewf (seh-wef)

Before – Lapatu (lah-pah-too)

Begin – Shki-Tuu-Aum (eek-hss-oot-moo-ah)

Beginning – Taka (tah-kah)

In the Beginning – Phe-Bnhu-Phe (eh-ph-whoo-nn-bee-eh-ph)

Behold – Shki-Nzu-Phe (eek-hss-ooh-zz-nn-eh-ph)

Being – She (shee)

Belly – Tihu (tee-whoo)

Belong – Sa (sah)

Besieged – Awq (awech)

Bestow (to bestow upon) – Jisu (jee-sue)

Bind – Shki-Phe-Shki (eek-hss-eh-ph-eek-hss)

Bird – Ess (esh)

Bite – Rewu (reh-woo)

Black – Kunah (koo-nah)

Black (to become black) – Eneh (en-eh)

Blessed/Blessing – Eos (ee-oh-ss)

Blood, Blood of – Phe-Aum-Nzu-Nzu (eh-ph-moo-ah-ooh-zz-nn-ooh-zz-nn)

Body – Zuhz (zoo-hez)

Book – Fa (fah)

Books – Qaz (qwaz)

Bond (bond heaven-earth) – Fuweh (foo-weh)

Born (one who was born) – Muh – (moo)

Bow – Aste (ash-the)

Bracelet – Semiru (seh-me-rue)

Break – Palas (pah-lass)

Breast – Khoki (koh-kee)

Breath, Living Breath - Aum-Hmu-Zhee (moo-ah-you-mmh-ha-eehzz)

Bride – Xau (shey-aw)

Bridle – Neq (nek)

Bright – Zhee-Lewhu-Aum (eehzz-ooh-wel-moo-ah)

Dwelling in the Brightness - Aum-Zhee-Aum (moo-ah-eehzz-moo-ah)

Bring forth - Hmu-Phe-Phe-Nzu (you-mmh-ha-eh-ph-eh-ph-ooh-zz-nn)

Bring – Wehdu (weh-do)

Bring to Naught - Ade La Bas Akahu (ah-day la ack-a-whoo)

Bronze – Ayes (ah-yes)

Brother – Zhee-Zhee-Aum (eehzz-moo-ah-moo-ah)

Brothers – Zhee-Zhee-Nzu-Aum (eehzz-eehzz-ooh-zz-nn-moo-ah)

Build – Mizuw (mee-zoo)

Building - Lewhu-Bnhu-Hmu (ooh-wel-whoo-nn-bee-you-mmh-ha)

Built - Nzu-Tuu-Phe-Aum (ooh-zz-nn-oot-eh-ph-moo-ah)

Burn, Burning - Zhee-Shki-Nzu-Phe-Bnhu (eehzz-eek-hss-ooh-zz-nn-eh-ph-whoo-nn-bee)

Business (Spirit of) Zhafu (zah-foo)

By - Aum-Tuu-Aum (moo-ah-oot-moo-ah)

Cage – Qupe (cue-peh)

Call, Called - Nzu-Nzu-Hmu (ooh-zz-nn-ooh-zz-nn-you-mmh-ha)

Called, Named - Shki-Bnhu-Aum (eek-hss-whoo-nn-bee-moo-ah)

Calm Down – Neled (neh-led)

Came – Ehf (eph)

Campaign – Goezh (go-ehz)

Carry – Wavat (wave-at)

Case – Umeh (you-meh)

Case of – Dinu (dee-new)

Cast = Hmu-Bnhu-Zhee-Shki (you-mmh-ha-whoo-nn-bee-eehzz-eek-hss)

Cast down = Hmu-Nzu-Zhee-Bnhu-Shki (you-mmh-ha-ooh-zz-nn-eehzz-whoo-nn-bee-eek-hss)

Cattle - Hmu-Aum-Nzu-Shki-Nzu (you-mmh-ha-moo-ah-ooh-zz-nn-eek-hss-ooh-zz-nn)

Cave - Shki-Hmu-Lewhu-Nzu-Zhee (eek-hss-you-mmh-ha-ooh-wel-ooh-zz-nn-eehzz)

Celestial Body – Mul-Karma (mool-kar-mah)

Center - Zhee-Bnhu-Zhee (eehzz-whoo-nn-bee-eehzz)

Chamber - Aum-Phe-Phe-Aum-Zhee (moo-ah-eh-ph-eh-ph-moo-ah-eehzz)

Change – A'Shki (ah-eek-hss)

Changed (turned into) – Tu (too)

Chant – Ji (jee)

Chariot/Car – Qw (qew)

Chariot (celestial chariot) – Iste (ish-tay)

Cheek – Kli (klee)

Child – Mteh (mm-the)

Children - Mha (muh-ha)

Chocolate – Lutu (loo-too)

Choice – Nami (nah-mee)

Choral Bands – Kaui (kah-you-ee)

Circle - Lewhu-Nzu-Phe-Zhee (ooh-wel-ooh-zz-nn-eh-ph-eehzz)

Citizens – Isze (ish-zeh)

City – Iszah (ish-za)

Claim – Rugu (roo-goo)

Clairvoyance – Anu (an-new)

Clay – Tedu (teh-doo)

Close (to draw near) – Qibusi (qwee-boo-see)

Clothed (to be clothed) – Lebu (leh-boo)

Clothed - Nzu-Nzu-Shki-Aum (ooh-zz-nn-ooh-zz-nn-eek-hss-moo-ah)

Come – Afuno (ah-foo-no)

Come - Aum-Hmu-Hmu (moo-ah-you-mmh-ha-you-mmh-ha)

Come Forth - Hmu-Hmu-Aum-Shki (you-mmh-ha-you-mmh-ha-moo-ah-eek-hss)

Comforter - Nzu-Bnhu-Nzu-Shki (ooh-zz-nn-whoo-nn-bee-ooh-zz-nn-eek-hss)

Command – Ksu (kah-soo)

Commanded – Ksu-Tuu (kah-soo)

Commanders – Sutaw (soo-tarw)

Commanding – Sute (soo-teh)

Compensate – Wano (wah-noh)

Concubine – Sintu (sin-too)

Conclude - Shki-Shki-Aum-Zhee-Shki (eek-hss-eek-hss-moo-ah-eehzz-eek-hss)

Confirming angels - Lewhu-Nzu-Nzu-Tuu (ooh-wel-ooh-zz-nn-ooh-zz-nn-oot)

Confine – Ulak (you-lack)

Confound - Phe-Lewhu-Nzu-Aum-Phe (eh-ph-ooh-wel-ooh-zz-nn-moo-ah-eh-ph)

Conquered – Dharma (thar-mah)

Container – Urno (er-noh)

Contents - Tuu-Nzu-Phe-Aum (oot-ooh-zz-nn-eh-ph-moo-ah)

Continual - Aum-Zhee-Aum-Zhee (moo-ah-eehzz-moo-ah-eehzz)

Continuance - Aum-Aum-Aum-Zhee-Aum (moo-ah-moo-ah-moo-ah-eehzz-moo-ah)

Contract – Rikto (ric-toh)

Convict – Kanoh (can-no) KANOH

Corner, Corners - Nzu-Phe-Phe-Lewhu-Aum-Hmu (ooh-zz-nn-eh-ph-eh-ph-ooh-wel-moo-ah-you-mmh-ha)

Corners - Shki-Tuu-Nzu-Tuu (eek-hss-oot-ooh-zz-nn-oot)

Corpse – Pisah (pee-sa)

Count (to count) – Mehno (meh-noh)

Count - Bnhu-Tuu-Tuu-Zhee-Hmu (whoo-nn-bee-oot-oot-eehzz-you-mmh-ha)

Course – Arunoh (ah-rue-no)

Covenant - Zhee-Shki-Aum-Tuu (eehzz-eek-hss-moo-ah-oot)

Cover, covered - Nzu-Shki-Nzu-Nzu-Hmu (ooh-zz-nn-eek-hss-ooh-zz-nn-ooh-zz-nn-you-mmh-ha)

Creation - Zhee-Nzu-Aum-Aum-Zhee (eehzz-ooh-zz-nn-moo-ah-moo-ah-eehzz)

Creator - Zhee-Aum-Aum-Zhee (eehzz-moo-ah-moo-ah-eehzz)

Crevice – Niudar (nee-you-dar)

Crow – Shki-Zhee-Phe (eek-hss-eehzz-eh-ph)

Crown(s) (object) - Aum-Zhee-Shki-Aum (moo-ah-eehzz-eek-hss-moo-ah)

Crown (to crown) - Aum-Zhee-Shki-Aum (moo-ah-eehzz-eek-hss-moo-ah)

Crown – Xijah (she-ja)

Cup, Cups - Nzu-Nzu-Shki-Shki (ooh-zz-nn-ooh-zz-nn-eek-hss-eek-hss) 7799

Cut – Pahro (pa-row)

Currency (money) – Kusam (koo-sam)

Curse – Ezoh (ezz-oh)

Cutting – Suni (soo-nee)

Daily – Ugiha (you-gee-ha)

Dangerous – Akna (ahk-na)

Dark (to be dark) – Euzha (ee-you-zha)

Dark place – Issio (ee-see-oh)

Darkness - Shki-Zhee-Nzu-Hmu-Aum (eek-hss-eehzz-ooh-zz-nn-you-mmh-ha-moo-ah)

Daughter - Zhee-Aum-Lewhu-Hmu-Nzu-Aum (eehzz-moo-ah-ooh-wel-you-mmh-ha-ooh-zz-nn-moo-ah)

Date – Shpu (sh-pu)

Day - Bnhu-Zhee-Bnhu-Nzu-Nzu (whoo-nn-bee-eehzz-whoo-nn-bee-ooh-zz-nn-ooh-zz-nn)

Dead – Mele (mel-lay)

Dead Person – Meleha (mel-lay-ha)

Death - Shki-Zhee-Shki-Zhee (eek-hss-eehzz-eek-hss-eehzz)

Decide (to render) – Pashi (pa-shee)

Decision – Turusi (too-roo-see)

Declare – Edou (edo-you) 𒄑𒀸𒃲

Deed/Deeds – Inahi (ee-na-ee) 𒌋𒀭𒌋

Deep Water – Phu (foo) 𒀀𒄑

Defeat – Ujan (you-jan) 𒄿𒀀𒋫

Demons (evil spirits) – Blku (blu-ku) 𒌋𒆜𒆜𒀭

Denounce – Tani (ta-nee) 𒀭𒋫𒀀𒌋

Departs – Olel (oh-lel) 𒅆𒆜𒆜

Deport – Umeh (you-may) 𒀭𒇺𒀀

Desire - Hmu-Ayaqox-Aum (you-mmh-ha-i-yah-quas-moo-ah) 𒀭𒆜𒌋𒄑𒀀𒍣𒈦

Destroy - Shki-Bnhu-Nzu (eek-hss-whoo-nn-bee-ooh-zz-nn) 𒈦𒌋𒌋

Destroy – Bhku (beh-ku) 𒌋𒄑𒆜𒀭

Destruction - Shki-Shki-Nzu (eek-hss-eek-hss-ooh-zz-nn) 𒈦𒈦𒌋

Devour - Nzu-aum-Zhee-Hmu (ooh-zz-nn-moo-ah-eehzz-you-mmh-ha) 𒌋𒌋𒌋𒀭𒀀

Diamond - Nzu-Hmu-Hmu-Zhee-Aum (ooh-zz-nn-you-mmh-ha-you-mmh-ha-eehzz-moo-ah) 𒌋𒀀𒀀𒀀𒈦

Die - Shki-Shki-Lewhu-Shki (eek-hss-eek-hss-ooh-wel-eek-hss) 𒈦𒈦𒉿𒈦

Difficult – Namsu (nahm-soo) 𒍣𒀭𒄑𒅆𒀭

Diminish – Seheru (seh-heh-roo) 𒅆𒄑𒀀𒊹𒀭

Dimension - *Shki-Shki-Nzu-Aum (eek-hss-eek-hss-ooh-zz-nn-moo-ah)*

Direction – *Nn (nn)*

Dirt - *Tuu-Shki-Bnhu (oot-eek-hss-whoo-nn-bee)*

Disease – *Fuhoh (few-oh)*

District – *Nahju (na-joo)*

Divide - *Phe-Nzu-Shki-Tuu (eh-ph-ooh-zz-nn-eek-hss-oot)*

Divine – *Ny/Ni (nigh)*

Divine Being – *Ninzuwu (nen-zoo-woo)*

Divinity – *Zuho (zoo-ho)*

Divining - *Aum-Phe-Tuu-Aum-Tuu (moo-ah-eh-ph-oot-moo-ah-oot)*

Do - *Phe-Zhee-Bnhu (eh-ph-eehzz-whoo-nn-bee)*

Dog - *Phe-Phe-Hwa (eh-ph-eh-ph-heh-wa)*

Dogs – *Hwa (heh-wa)*

Door - *Lewhu-Shki-Lewhu (ooh-wel-eek-hss-ooh-wel)*

Dove – *Yukwa (you-qwa)*

Dragon - *Aum-Zhee-Phe-Aum-Aum (moo-ah-eehzz-eh-ph-moo-ah-moo-ah)*

Dragons – *Su (soo)*

Draw near – *Qit (qw-eet)*

Dream - Phe-Aum-Aum-Bnhu (eh-ph-moo-ah-moo-ah-whoo-nn-bee)

Dreams – Ryu (rlee-you)

Drink – Anvah (an-vah)

Drinks (beer) – Kashi (kah-shee)

Dust – Uepru (you-ep-purr)

Dwell – Teeho (tee-hoh)

Dwelling – Bhso (bah-soh)

Dwelling Place – Manazazu (man-ah-za-zoo)

Eagle - Aum-Bnhu-Aum (moo-ah-whoo-nn-bee-moo-ah)

Ear – Uzum (you-zum)

Earth (spirit of/cosmic) – Zuchi (zoo-chee)

Earth - Shki-Lewhu-Zhee (eek-hss-ooh-wel-eehzz)

Earth (planet) – Mazu (mah-tsu)

Eat - Tuu-Shki (oot-eek-hss)

Ecstasy – Qox (qaus)

Ego - Aum-Aum-Shki-Zhee-Tuu (moo-ah-moo-ah-eek-hss-eehzz-oot)

Ego (false) – Krystz (chris-tez)

Eight/Eighth – Lewhu (ooh-wel)

Elixir - Aum-Nzu-Aum-Hmu (moo-ah-ooh-zz-nn-moo-ah-you-mmh-ha)

Empty - Shki-Aum-Phe-Nzu-Nzu (eek-hss-moo-ah-eh-ph-ooh-zz-nn-ooh-zz-nn)

Enchanting - Tuu-Tuu-Hmu-Aum (oot-oot-you-mmh-ha-moo-ah)

Encourage – Tehkul (teh-kool)

Enemy – Ahonu (ah-ho-new)

Enemies – Jex (jeh-xch)

Energy - Aum-Aum-Zhee-Tuu (moo-ah-moo-ah-eehzz-oot)

Enjoy – Zonget (zhon-get)

Enlarge – Supir (soo-peer)

Enter - Bnhu-Tuu-Bnhu-Tuu (whoo-nn-bee-oot-whoo-nn-bee-oot)

Entered – Erimu (eh-ree-moo)

Entire - Hmu-Shki-Shki (you-mmh-ha-eek-hss-eek-hss)

Entity - Hmu-Zhee-Zhee-Aum-Phe (you-mmh-ha-eehzz-eehzz-moo-ah-eh-ph)

Envelope – Sazolu (sah-zo-loo)

Evoking - Hmu-Shki-Shki-Nzu (you-mmh-ha-eek-hss-eek-hss-ooh-zz-nn)

Escape – Nasudu (nah-soo-doo)

Established – Kinu (kee-new)

Equal (or to make equal) – Masehlu (ma-say-loo)

Ever – Inuha (ee-new-ha)

Every – Nabu (nah-boo)

Evil Eye (look at malevolently) – Nekes (nek-ess)

Evil – Aho (ah-ho)

Eye – Evaki (ee-vah-kee)

Excavation – Keho (keh-ho)

Excite - Phe-Phe-Nzu-Hmu-Tuu (eh-ph-eh-ph-ooh-zz-nn-you-mmh-ha-oot)

Excrement - Phe-Lewhu-Tuu-Tuu (eh-ph-ooh-wel-oot-oot)

Executed (to be executed) – Daho (dah-ho)

Exit – Atutoh (ah-too-toe)

Experience - Shki-Aum-Phe-Aum (eek-hss-moo-ah-eh-ph-moo-ah)

Explain - Tuu-Zhee-Nzu-Phe (oot-eehzz-ooh-zz-nn-eh-ph)

Explode - Zhee-Tuu-Tuu (eehzz-oot-oot)

Extinguish – Sqolu (ss-qwo-lu)

Eye - Aum-Zhee-Tuu-Bnhu-Zhee (moo-ah-eehzz-oot-whoo-nn-bee-eehzz)

Face – Pir (peer)

Face - Zhee-Tuu-Phe-Bnhu (eehzz-oot-eh-ph-whoo-nn-bee)

Faceless - Bnhu-Zhee-Tuu-Phe-Bnhu (whoo-nn-bee-eehzz-oot-eh-ph-whoo-nn-bee)

Fade - Phe-Lewhu-Bnhu-Tuu (eh-ph-ooh-wel-whoo-nn-bee-oot)

Faith – Anahit (an-nah-het)

Fall – Makatu (mah-ka-too)

Falsehood – Saras (sa-rass)

Family – Zir (zeer)

Fangs - Zhee-Shki-Aum (eehzz-eek-hss-moo-ah)

Far – Ruku (roo-koo)

Fashioned – Ibatano (ee-bah-ta-no)

Fat - Hmu-Tuu (you-mmh-ha-oot)

Fate – Sitti (see-tee)

Father - Aum-Zhee-Aum-Lewhu (moo-ah-eehzz-moo-ah-ooh-wel) moo-ah-eehzz-moo-ah-ooh-wel)

Father – Azaho (ah-za-ho)

Father of – Azahozu (ah-za-ho-zoo)

Favorite – Mehgru (may-grew)

Fear – Huun (hoone)

Fear - Shki-Aum-Nzu-Shki (eek-hss-moo-ah-ooh-zz-nn-eek-hss)

Feel - Hmu-Hmu-Aum (you-mmh-ha-you-mmh-ha-moo-ah)

Female – Nu (noo)

Flee – Ahujo (ah-whoo-jo)

Fifth – Hato (ha-toh)

Fifty – Bnhu-El (whoo-nn-bee-ehl)

Field – Eqa (ee-qwa)

Fighting - Nzu-Tuu-Tuu-Phe (ooh-zz-nn-oot-oot-eh-ph)

Fire - Nzu-Zhee-Nzu (ooh-zz-nn-eehzz-ooh-zz-nn)

Fire (cosmic) – Wutzki (woo-tss-skee)

First - Zhee-Zhee (eehzz-eehzz)

Fish – Hako (ha-koh)

Five – Bnhu (whoo-nn-bee)

Five (5, 51) - Bnhu-Zhee (whoo-nn-bee-eehzz)

Flaming - Nzu-Zhee-Nzu-Phe (ooh-zz-nn-eehzz-ooh-zz-nn-eh-ph)

Flood – Tahneh (tah-nay)

Flow - Nzu-Hmu-Tuu-Phe (ooh-zz-nn-you-mmh-ha-oot-eh-ph)

Fly - Nzu-Nzu-Phe (ooh-zz-nn-ooh-zz-nn-eh-ph)

Food – Subuso (soo-boo-soh)

Foolish - Phe-Tuu-Tuu-Phe (eh-ph-oot-oot-eh-ph)

Foot – Pahgir (pa-geer)

For – Bohi (bow-hee)

Forbidden – Ikko (ee-koh)

Force (by force) – Ehuqo (eh-hoo-qwo)

Foremost – Nulo (new-loh)

Forest/Forests – Poh (po)

Forever – Dari (da-ree)

Forget = lewhu-nzu-nzu-phe

Forgive – Vh (vuh)

Fortification – Alhalsu (al-hal-soo)

Fortresses – Lunoho (loo-no-ho)

Fought – Imahato (ee-ma-ha-toe)

Foul - Shki-Bnhu-Shki (eek-hss-whoo-nn-bee-eek-hss)

Found - Phe-Phe-Hmu-Tuu (eh-ph-eh-ph-you-mmh-ha-oot)

Foundation – Ixchel (iss-chel)

Four – Hmu (you-mmh-ha)

Four (4, 14) - Zhee-Hmu (eehzz-you-mmh-ha)

Free - Aum-Tuu-Tuu-Phe-Bnhu (moo-ah-oot-oot-eh-ph-whoo-nn-bee)

Friend/Friends – Zaso (zha-soh)

From - Phe-Lewhu-Lewhu-Phe (eh-ph-ooh-wel-ooh-wel-eh-ph)

Front - Nzu-Shki-Lewhu-Bnhu (ooh-zz-nn-eek-hss-ooh-wel-whoo-nn-bee)

Furniture - Numah (new-ma)

Garment – Tugsha (tug-shah)

Gate – Haki (ha-kee)

Gatekeeper – Hahun (ha-hoon)

Gathering - Nzu-Hmu-Lewhu-Tuu-Nzu (ooh—nn-you-

mmh-ha-ooh-wel-oot-ooh-zz-nn) 4乙ᕁᕁ

Gave (he/she gave) – Menoh (meh-noh)

Genius - Aum-Tuu-Nzu-Hmu-Phe-Phe (moo-ah-oot-ooh-

zz-nn-you-mh-ha-eh-ph-eh-ph)

Gentle – Soh (so)

Ghost - Aum-Aum-Zhee (moo-ah-moo-ah-eehzz)

Ghosts – Wuz (wooz)

Gift – Igisumo (ehg-ee-soo-mo)

Give – Nasoho (na-so-oh)

Go – Dukla (duke-lah)

God Aum-Zhee-Aum-Zhee-Aum (moo-ah-eehzz-moo-ah-

eehzz-moo-ah)

Goddess - Aum-Aum-Zhee-Zhee-Aum (moo-ah-moo-ah-

eehzz-eehzz-moo-ah)

Going - Phe-Aum-Nzu-Phe (eh-ph-moo-ah-ooh-zz-nn-eh-

ph)

Going (going out) – Jitu (jee-too)

Gold – Nuit (noot)

Good – Iah (eey-ah)

Good Fortune – Ataensic (ah-ta-in-sic)

Goodness – Ama (ah-mah)

Glowing – Dhqi (deh-kee)

Grain – Semo (she-mo)

Grant - Tuu-Shki-Tuu-Zhee (oot-eek-hss-oot-eehzz)

Gravity - Bnhu-Zhee-Zhee-Tuu-Phe-Phe (whoo-nn-bee-eehzz-eehzz-oot-eh-ph-eh-ph)

Great - Zhee-Phe-Lewhu-Hmu-Lewhu (eehzz-eh-ph-ooh-wel-you-mmh-ha-ooh-wel)

Green - Aum-Hmu-Hmu-Zhee-Tuu (moo-ah-you-mmh-ha-you-mmh-ha-eehzz-oot)

Greetings – Wafubeh (wa-foo-bay)

Ground – Nud (nood)

Guard – Nasaro (na-sa-ro)

‡

Hair - Lewhu-Bnhu-Bnhu-Phe (ooh-wel-whoo-nn-bee-whoo-nn-bee-eh-ph)

Hand – Zato (za-toh)

Hang – Alah (ah-lah)

Happiness - Shki-Phe-Nzu-Nzu-Phe (eek-hss-eh-ph-ooh-zz-nn-ooh-zz-nn-eh-ph)

Happy - Phe-Hmu-Hmu-Tuu-Phe (eh-ph-you-mmh-ha-you-mmh-ha-oot-eh-ph)

Hard - Phe-Tuu-Tuu-Hmu-Phe (eh-ph-oot-oot-you-mmh-ha-eh-ph)

Harlot - Shki-Aum-Tuu-Zhee (eek-hss-moo-ah-oot-eehzz)

Harmony – Nunnehi (nun-nay-hee)

Harvest – Olokunsu (oh-lo-kun-sue)

Has – Akna (ack-nah)

Hate - Shki-Zhee-Tuu-Aum (eek-hss-eehzz-oot-moo-ah)

Have, Having - Bnhu-Tuu-Nzu-Nzu-Shki (whoo-nn-bee-oot-ooh-zz-nn-ooh-zz-nn-eek-hss)

Head - Lewhu-Aum-Aum-Bnhu (ooh-wel-moo-ah-moo-ah-whoo-nn-bee)

Head (leader) - Zhee-Aum-Nzu-Nzu-Aum (eehzz-moo-ah-ooh-zz-nn-ooh-zz-nn-moo-ah)

Healing - Hmu-Aum-Aum-Phe-Zhee-Shki (you-mmh-ha-moo-ah-moo-ah-eh-ph-eehzz-eek-hss)

Health - Phe-Phe-Shki (eh-ph-eh-ph-eek-hss)

Hear - Bnhu-Lewhu-Phe-Lewhu (whoo-nn-bee-ooh-wel-eh-ph-ooh-wel)

Heart – Vesna (ves-nah)

Heat - Tuu-Tuu-Nzu-Nzu-Zhee (oot-oot-ooh-zz-nn-ooh-zz-nn-eehzz)

Heaven - Aum-Aum-Shki-Hmu-Phe (moo-ah-moo-ah-eek-hss-you-mmh-ha-eh-ph)

Heavens – Auset (awh-set)

Heavenly (the heavenly one) – Onazu (oh-na-zoo)

Heavy – Asoh (ah-so)

Heir – Zwato (zz-wa-toh)

Help – Yessi (yeh-see)

Hell - Phe-Hmu-Shki-Aum-Aum (eh-ph-you-mmh-ha-eek-hss-moo-ah-moo-ah)

Herb – Owui (oh-woo-ee)

Heritage – Shiva (shee-va)

Hide – Matti (mat-tee)

Hidden - Tuu-Tuu-Nzu-Phe-Nzu (oot-oot-ooh-zz-nn-eh-ph-ooh-zz-nn)

High - Phe-Hmu-Tuu-Lewhu-Lewhu-Nzu (eh-ph-you-mmh-ha-oot-ooh-wel-ooh-wel-ooh-zz-nn)

Hire – Agaro (ah-ga-ro)

Hold – Kalu (Kah-loo)

Holy - Aum-Aum-Hmu-Lewhu (moo-ah-moo-ah-you-mmh-ha-ooh-wel)

Home – Esharo (eh-sha-ro)

Honesty – Sekhmet (sek-mhet)

Honor – Zorya (zore-yah)

Horn – Qnu (qwa-noo)

Horse – Vahuw (va-whew)

Hour – Hthah (heh-th-ah)

House – Shki-Aum-Shki-Phe-Aum (eek-hss-moo-ah-eek-hss-eh-ph-moo-ah)

How – Lewhu-Nzu-Nzu (ooh-wel-ooh-zz-nn-ooh-zz-nn)

Human – Shki-Hmu-Hmu-Phe (eek-hss-you-mmh-ha-you-mmh-ha-eh-ph)

Hungry – Hmu-Phe-Phe-Shki-Shki (you-mmh-ha-eh-ph-eh-ph-eek-hss-eek-hss)

Hunt – Tuu-Shki-Shki-Tuu-Tuu (oot-eek-hss-eek-hss-oot-oot)

Hunter – Xisha (shee-sha)

Husk – Tuu-Tuu-Nzu-Tuu-Phe (oot-oot-ooh-zz-nn-oot-eh-ph)

I – Aum-Tuu-Tuu-Phe (moo-ah-oot-oot-eh-ph)

Idea – Zhnuho (zhoo-ho)

211

Illness - Nzu-Tuu-Phe-Phe-Bnhu (ooh-zz-nn-oot-eh-ph-eh-ph-whoo-nn-bee)

Illuminating - Phe-Phe-Shki-Aum-Tuu (eh-ph-eh-ph-eek-hss-moo-ah-oot)

Imagination - Nzu-Phe-Phe-Hmu-Shki (ooh-zz-nn-eh-ph-eh-ph-you-mmh-ha-eek-hss)

Immediately – Khuto (qwu-toh)

Immortal – Zu (zoo)

Immortal – Xiwangmu (Shee-warng-moo)

Impose – Umajo (you-ma-joh)

Impregnate – Vnuho (ven-you-ho)

Imprison –Yuqw (you-qweh)

In – Toci (toh-she)

In - Shki-Hmu-Hmu (eek-hss-you-mmh-ha-you-mmh-ha)

Incantation – Utoh (you-toh)

Incense - Hmu-Nzu-Hmu-Tuu (you-mmh-ha-ooh-zz-nn-you-mmh-ha-oot)

Incidentally - Aum-Shki-Zhee-Nzu-Tuu (moo-ah-eek-hss-eehzz-ooh-zz-nn-oot)

Increase - Zhee-Tuu-Hmu-Nzu-Aum (eehzz-oot-you-mmh-ha-ooh-zz-nn-moo-ah)

Infinite, infinity - Aum-Hmu-Hmu-Aum-Tuu (moo-ah-you-mmh-ha-you-mmh-ha-moo-ah-oot)

Information - Tuu-Aum-Bnhu (oot-moo-ah-whoo-nn-bee)

Inner - Phe-Tuu-Zhee-Phe (eh-ph-oot-eehzz-eh-ph)

Innocent – Vitaho (vee-ta-ho)

Insane - Zhee-Aum-Shki-Nzu-Tuu-Nzu (eehzz-moo-ah-eek-hss-ooh-zz-nn-oot-ooh-zz-nn)

Instinct – Tashnit (tash-knit)

Intuition - Shki-Aum-Aum-Zhee-Tuu (eek-hss-moo-ah-moo-ah-eehzz-oot)

Invoking - Zhee-Aum-Tuu-Bnhu-Zhee (eehzz-moo-ah-oot-whoo-nn-bee-eehzz)

Inward - Shki-Hmu-Hmu-Zhee-Phe (eek-hss-you-mmh-ha-you-mmh-ha-eehzz-eh-ph)

Iron - Phe-Phe-Phe (eh-ph-eh-ph-eh-ph)

Is – Muzi (moo-zee)

It - Tuu-Aum-Tuu-Tuu-Shki-Phe (oot-moo-ah-oot-oot-eek-hss-eh-ph)

It is done - Aum-Zhee-Hmu-Phe-Shki-Tuu (moo-ah-eehzz-you-mmh-ha-eh-ph-eek-hss-oot)

Ivory – Zuka (zoo-kah)

A

Jackal - Hmu-Aum-Zhee-Phe (you-mmh-ha-moo-ah-eehzz-eh-ph)

Jade – Vjoh-Aum (veh-jo-moo-ah)

Jealous – Wahno (wa-noh)

Jewel - Aum-Phe-Hmu-Zhee (moo-ah-eh-ph-you-mmh-ha-eehzz)

Journey – Tuzo (too-zoh)

Joy - Aum-Hmu-Hmu (moo-ah-you-mmh-ha-you-mmh-ha)

Joyfully – Sidhas (sede-has)

Judge – Kohuz (ko-whooz)

Judgement – Kohuzi (ko-whooz-ee)

Judges – Iwauzo (ee-wa-you-zoh)

Judging – Bazso (baz-so)

Juice - Shki-Phe-Hmu-Phe (eek-hss-eh-ph-you-mmh-ha-eh-ph)

Jump – Vozoj (vo-zog)

Juniper – Lzul (leh-zz-you'll)

Jupiter - Aum-Zhee-Aum (moo-ah-eehzz-moo-ah)

Jupiter (spirit of) – Koqw (ko-qweh)

Jury – Buhota (boo-ho-tah)

Justice – Ruho (roo-ho)

Keep – Osqo (ahs-koh)

Keeping – Osqui (ahs-que-ee)

Kennel – Hyol (heh-yowl)

Kept – Asqo (ash-koh)

Kettle – Tsuloh (tss-you-loh)

Key – Sukof (soo-kofh)

Keys – Aum-Neh (moo-ah-neh)

Kick – Wsu (weh-soo)

Kicked – Wsuho (weh-soo-oh)

Kill – Lvnoh (lev-noh)

Kind – Okuk (oh-kook)

Kindness – Okuko (oh-kook-oh)

Kindred – Xiwuko (she-woo-koh)

King – Warunoh (war-you-no)

Kingdom – Warosu (war-oh-soo)

Kings – Waruna (war-you-nah)

Kingship – Waroh (war-oh)

Kiss – Ujinoh (you-gee-no)

Kitchen – Viwo (vee-woh)

Knife - Shki-Phe-Phe-Tuu (eek-hss-eh-ph-eh-ph-oot)

Knight - Hmu-Phe-Aum-Phe-Tuu (you-mmh-ha-eh-ph-moo-ah-eh-ph-oot)

Know – Namaka (naye-ma-kah)

Knowledge – Mudutu (moo-doo-too)

Labyrinth - Aum-Tuu-Tuu-Phe (moo-ah-oot-oot-eh-ph)

Lack – Samo (sah-mo)

Lady - Aum-Zhee-Zhee (moo-ah-eehzz-eehzz)

Lady – Zaramama (Za-rah-ma-ma)

Land – Matumo (mah-too-mo)

Language - Phe-Hmu-Bnhu-Tuu (eh-ph-you-mmh-ha-whoo-nn-bee-oot)

Last - Shki-Aum-Phe-Phe-Tuu (eek-hss-moo-ah-eh-ph-eh-ph-oot)

Laugh - Tuu-Hmu-Nzu (oot-you-mmh-ha-ooh-zz-nn)

Law – Yohak (yo-hok)

Lead – Oedu (oh-ee-do)

Learn – Lamadu (la-ma-do)

Leave – Ezebu (eh-zay-boo)

Leg - Shki-Nzu-Nzu-Hmu (eek-hss-ooh-zz-nn-ooh-zz-nn-you-mmh-ha)

Leviathan - Zhee-Hmu-Phe-Aum-Zhee (eehzz-you-mmh-ha-eh-ph-moo-ah-eehzz)

Liar – Saroh (sah-row)

Lie Down – Utulu (you-too-loo)

Life – Napis (nah-pees)

Life - Aum-Nzu-Nzu-Aum-Zhee (moo-ah-ooh-zz-nn-ooh-zz-nn-moo-ah-eehzz)

Life – Inanna (eh-nah-nah)

Light – Joh (Jo)

Lightning – Baraqo (ba-ra-kqo)

Lightning flash - Aum-Shki-Bnhu-Aum (moo-ah-eek-hss-whoo-nn-bee-moo-ah)

Like - Zhee-Nzu-Nzu (eehzz-ooh-zz-nn-ooh-zz-nn)

Lip – Sapto (sap-toh)

Live – Sekinek (Say-key-nec)

Liver – Kobito (ko-bee-toe)

Lock – Sikiro (see-keer-oh)

Look – Nakoko (nah-ko-ko)

Lord – Bei (bay)

Lord - Shki-Aum-Nzu-Phe-Zhee (eek-hss-moo-ah-ooh-zz-nn-eh-ph-eehzz)

Lose – Jalqo (jahl-qwo)

Lost - Nzu-Phe-Nzu (ooh-zz-nn-eh-ph-ooh-zz-nn)

Loud - Hmu-Aum-Hmu (you-mmh-ha-moo-ah-you-mmh-ha)

Love - Aum-Zhee-Bnhu (moo-ah-eehzz-whoo-nn-bee)

Love (romantic) – Oshun (oh-shoon)

Low - Shki-Nzu-Nzu-Tuu (eek-hss-ooh-zz-nn-ooh-zz-nn-oot)

Lower – Salpu (sal-poo)

Loyalty - Aum-Zhee-Bnhu-Tuu (moo-ah-eehzz-whoo-nn-bee-oot)

Lust - Aum-Tuu-Zhee (moo-ah-oot-eehzz)

Made – Ezeboh (ehz-eh-bo)

Magician - Zhee-Aum-Tuu-Phe (eehzz-moo-ah-oot-eh-ph)

Magic - Aum-Zhee-Tuu-Hmu-Aum (moo-ah-eehzz-oot-you-mmh-ha-moo-ah)

Magus - Zhee-Aum-Bnhu (eehzz-moo-ah-whoo-nn-bee)

Make - Aum-Shki-Shki-Aum-Tuu (moo-ah-eek-hss-eek-hss-moo-ah-oot)

Male – Ziko (zee-koh)

Man – Ohuz (oh-whooz)

Mankind – Quhowa (qwa-ho-wa)

Mars - Aum-Bnhu-Zhee (moo-ah-whoo-nn-bee-eehzz)

Mars (Dragon of) – Buhqz (boo-heh-cuz)

Matter - Zhee-Tuu-Tuu (eehzz-oot-oot)

Me – Uta – (ew-tah)

Means - Hmu-Tuu-Zhee (you-mmh-ha-oot-eehzz)

Medicine - Bnhu-Aum-Nzu-Nzu (whoo-nn-bee-moo-ah-ooh-zz-nn-ooh-zz-nn)

Memory – Xian (she-an)

Mercury - Aum-Tuu-Tuu-Shki-Thoth (moo-ah-oot-oot-eek-hss Thoth)

Mercury (spirit of) – Aixu (ay-eye-zoo)

Message – Wuru (woo-ru)

Messenger – Nidaba (nee-da-bah)

Metal/Metals – Zagoyu (za-go-you)

Middle –Inofu (ee-no-foo)

Mind - Hmu-Aum-Shki-Hmu (you-mmh-ha-moo-ah-eek-hss-you-mmh-ha)

Miracle – Issinoh (ee-ss-ee-no)

Miraculous – Isis (eye-sis)

Mist – Imbaru (em-ba-roo)

Month – Warhum (wahr-humm)

Moon (Dragon of) – Istu (ish-too)

Moon - Aum-Istu-Zhee (moo-ah-ish-too-eehzz)

Mother - Aum-Zhee-Aum-Tuu (moo-ah-eehzz-moo-ah-oot)

Mother – Uwuwu (you-woo-woo)

Mound – Eduku (eh-doo-koo)

Mount (to mount) – Sahatu (sa-ha-too)

Mountain – Kasoh (ka-soh)

Mountains – Ursano (uhr-sa-no)

Mouth - Tuu-Tuu-Hmu (oot-oot-you-mmh-ha)

Moving - Aum-Hmu-Tuu-Nzu (moo-ah-you-mmh-ha-oot-ooh-zz-nn)

Mouth – Nakuho (na-koo-ho)

Music - Hmu-Bnhu-Hmu-Tuu (you-mmh-ha-whoo-nn-bee-you-mmh-ha-oot)

My – Aine (iaw-neh)

Mystical - Shki-Nzu-Nzu (eek-hss-ooh-zz-nn-ooh-zz-nn)

Name – Swafu (swa-foo)

Nature – Lucxh (loo-sigh)

Near – Buwas (boo-wass)

Netherworld – Liseto (lee-she-toe)

Nine – Shki (eek-hss)

Ninth – Tiso (tee-so)

No – Ohu (oh-who)

Nose – Azih (ah-zee)

Not – Pehnu (peh-new)

Now – Gama (gah-ma)

Nurse – Wamifo (wah-mee-foh)

Oath – Namsoh (nahm-so)

Obey – Yhar (yeh-har)

Ocean – Watah (wa-ta)

Of – Yhi (yeh-hee)

Offerings – Uyosu (you-yo-soo)

Oil – Iazu (ee-ah-zoo)

Old – Takmeh (tawc-may)

One – Zhee (zee)

Open – Zahjo (za-jo)

Orchard – Sojik (so-jeek)

Ornament – Ittu (eet-too)

Overcome – Kasado (ka-sa-doh)

Overturn – Kutu (koo-too)

Paid – Opa (oh-pa)

Palace – Aqo (ah-ko)

Pain - Bnhu-Shki-Tuu (whoo-nn-bee-eek-hss-oot)

Part – Marama (mah-ra-ma)

Passion – Shintai (sh-in-tie)

Peace – Wohpe (who-pay)

Penalty – Jvun (je-voon)

Pentacle - Tuu-Tuu-Aum (oot-oot-moo-ah)

Perception - Aum-Nzu-Phe-Phe (moo-ah-ooh-zz-nn-eh-ph-eh-ph)

Perfect – Gitmo (get-mo)

Permitted - Aum-Hmu (moo-ah-you-mmh-ha)

Personality – Zeemah (zee-ma)

Phoenix - Hmu-Phe-Zhee-Phe-Phe (you-mmh-ha-eh-ph-eehzz-eh-ph-eh-ph)

Physician – Iazu (ee-ah-zoo)

Pierce - Nzu-Nzu-Hmu-Phe (ooh-zz-nn-ooh-zz-nn-you-mmh-ha-eh-ph)

Pig – Sahu (sa-whoo)

Place – Yarufa (ya-roo-fa)

Planet - *Shki-Aum-Tuu-Bnhu (eek-hss-moo-ah-oot-whoo-nn-bee)*

Plant - *Aum-Tuu-Tuu-Phe (moo-ah-oot-oot-eh-ph)*

Pleasure - *Phe-Tuu-Tuu-Phe (eh-ph-oot-oot-eh-ph)*

Plow - *Eresu (eh-reh-sue)*

Plunge – *Salu (sa-loo)*

Poison - *Lewhu-Phe-Zhee (ooh-wel-eh-ph-eehzz)*

Positive - *Shki-Tuu-Hmu (eek-hss-oot-you-mmh-ha)*

Possession - *Shki-Shki-Shki-Tuu (eek-hss-eek-hss-eek-hss-oot)*

Potential - *Shki-Nzu (eek-hss-ooh-zz-nn)*

Poured - *Sabuho (sa-boo-ho)*

Power – *Mahzew (ma-zooh)*

Power -*Lewhu-Aum-Zhee (ooh-wel-moo-ah-eehzz)*

Powerful – *Sepsu (sep-soo)*

Praise – *Freya (fray-yah)*

Precious – *Nisiqtu (nii-seek-too)*

Presence – *Mahro (mah-ro)*

Priest - *Aum-Zhee-Phe (moo-ah-eehzz-eh-ph)*

224

Priestess Ukavo (you-ka-vo)

Prince – Iwayo (ee-wa-yo)

Princess – Iwaya (ee-wa-ya)

Proceed – Zanuboh (za-new-bow)

Property – Izehu (eye-zeh-whoo)

Prophet (seer) – Nocoh (no-coh)

Prosperity – Sharra Itu (shar-rah-ee-too)

Protect, do protection - Aum-Aum-Phe-Hmu (moo-ah-moo-ah-eh-ph-you-mmh-ha)

Protects – Adahes (ah-da-es)

Pull – Baho (ba-ho)

Purple - Shki-Tuu-Phe (eek-hss-oot-eh-ph)

Pure/Purity – Mayahuel (ma-jah-wel)

Put – Fafo (fah-fo)

Qualify – Uhmbu (umm-boo)

Quality – Mwoh (mwa-oh)

Quantity – Opawk (oh-pahk)

Quarrel – Asisso (ahs-iss-oh)

Queen – Nohuk (no-hook)

Question – Rinoho (ree-no-ho)

Questions – Kaws (qawss)

Quick – Haq (hauq)

Quickly – Artupo (ar-too-po)

Quiet – Suhu (soo-hoo)

Radiate – Honshazeshonen (hon-sha-zay-show-nen)

Rain - Shki-Aum-Phe-Phe-Nzu (eek-hss-moo-ah-eh-ph-eh-ph-ooh-zz-nn)

Raise - Vlu (velw-you)

Rags – Karro (car-row)

Ramp – Gyu (geh-you)

Rare – Aqru (ahk-rue)

Reach –Sada (sa-da)

Reality – Sojobo (soh-jo-bo)

Receive – Maharu (ma-ha-roo)

Red – Sandu (san-doo)

Red - Aum-Nzu-Phe-Hmu (moo-ah-ooh-zz-nn-eh-ph-you-mmh-ha)

Regions – Shulim (shoo-leem)

Rejoice – Hadu (ha-do)

Release – Jakis (jah-kiss)

Religion - Lewhu-Nzu-Nzu-Bnhu (ooh-wel-ooh-zz-nn-ooh-zz-nn-whoo-nn-bee)

Remember – Sol (sole)

Remnant - Hmu-Phe-Tuu (you-mmh-ha-eh-ph-oot)

Remove – Tebu (teh-boo)

Render – Gyawl (ge-yall)

Reorganize – Anao (an-ah-oh)

Request – Eresu (eh-reh-soo)

Rest – Sittu (see-too)

Return – Taru (ta-roo)

Return - Zhee-Shki-Tuu-Tuu (eehzz-eek-hss-oot-oot)

Resurrect – Hecate (hek-ah-tay)

Resurrection – Hecate (hek-ah-tay)

Revealed - Tuu-Tuu-Phe (oot-oot-eh-ph)

Rib – Tiomo (tee-oh-mo)

Ride – Zakuno (za-koo-no)

Ring - Aum-Zhee-Phe-Tuu (moo-ah-eehzz-eh-ph-oot)

Rings – Yeno (yeh-no)

Rise - Tuu-Phe-Phe-Hmu (oot-eh-ph-eh-ph-you-mmh-ha)

Ritual - Aum-Tuu-Nzu (moo-ah-oot-ooh-zz-nn)

Rites – Belet (beh-let)

River – Margidah (mar-gee-da)

Road – Harano (ha-ran-oh)

Roam – Nojuki (no-joo-kee)

Rob – Visho (vee-sho)

Rope – Asanu (ah-sa-new)

Ruby – Yarahhu (ya-ra-hoo)

Ruin – Opewo (oh-poo-oh)

Rush – Boh (bo)

Sad – Hef (heft)

Safe – Denyo (den-yo)

Sanctum – Barag (ba-rag)

Saturn – Shiho (shee-ho)

Saturn (Dragon of) – Quf (koof)

Save – Eteru (eh-the-roo)

Saying – Izza (ee-zah)

Sea – Watah (wah-tah)

Seal – Kunuk (koo-nook)

Seat – Mubi (moo-bee)

Second – Ganoto (ga-no-toh)

See – Camazotz (ka-mah-zots)

Seed – Zanik (za-neek)

Seer – Yotoh (yo-toh)

Self- Maat (migh-ot)

Seller – Nadoro (na-door-oh)

Sent – Issaho (iss-sa-ho)

Serpent – Noga (no-gah)

Set – Sakanu (sa-ka-new)

Seven – Nzu (ooh-zz-nn)

Seventh – Sebu (seh-boo)

Shade – Sillu (see-loo)

Shadow - Bnhu-Hmu-Zhee (whoo-nn-bee-you-mmh-ha-eehzz)

Sharpen – Selu (seh-loo)

Shine – Augo (au-go)

Shines – Amaja (ah-mah-jah)

Ship – Kehva (kay-va)

Sick – Zaros (zah-rohs)

Side – Ubaw (you-bau)

Sieze – Otoyu (oh-toe-you)

Sigil - Zhee-Aum-Nzu (eehzz-moo-ah-ooh-zz-nn)

Sign - Shki-Bnhu (eek-hss-whoo-nn-bee)

Silent - Zhee-Tuu-Phe-Phe-Tuu (eehzz-oot-eh-ph-eh-ph-oot)

Silver – Tsuki (tss-you-kee)

Sin – Basha (ba-sha)

Sing – Holu (hole-loo)

Singer – Holuna (hole-loo-na)

Single – Ebi (eh-bee)

Sister – Gahu (ga-whoo)

Sit – Wito (weh-toh)

Six – Pha (eh-ph)

Skin - Aum-Tuu-Tuu-Bnhu (moo-ah-oot-oot-whoo-nn-bee)

Slave - Tuu-Tuu-Phe (oot-oot-eh-ph)

Small - Tuu-Phe-Phe-Hmu (oot-eh-ph-eh-ph-you-mmh-ha)

Smoke - Hmu-Shki-Zhee (you-mmh-ha-eek-hss-eehzz)

Snakes – Emu (ee-moo)

Soldier – Zanuhi (za-new-ee)

Son – Muruh (moo-roo)

Son - Aum-Tuu-Phe (moo-ah-oot-eh-ph)

Sorcery - Lewhu-Bnhu-Aum (ooh-wel-whoo-nn-bee-moo-ah)

Sorrow – Hef (heft)

Soul - Uta – (ew-tah)

Speak – Mekau (me-kaw)

Sphere - Shki-Zhee-Zhee (eek-hss-eehzz-eehzz)

Spider - Aum-Bnhu-Nzu-Nzu (moo-ah-whoo-nn-bee-ooh-zz-nn-ooh-zz-nn)

Spirit/Spirits – Wu (woo)

Spirit World – La'atzu (la-at-zoo)

Spoil – Safu (sa-foo)

Spoke – Matu (ma-too)

Square - Aum-Tuu-Nzu (moo-ah-oot-ooh-zz-nn)

Stand - Nzu-Phe-Phe (ooh-zz-nn-eh-ph-eh-ph)

Stand – Zuzu (zoo-zoo)

Star - Zhee-Shki-Tuu-Phe (eehzz-eek-hss-oot-eh-ph)

Sting - Tuu-Tuu-Phe (oot-oot-eh-ph)

Stir – Dalahu (da-la-hoo)

Stole Qriso (chriss-oh)

Stone – Nuab (new-ab)

Stop – Fuwani (foo-wa-nee)

Stop - Phe-Nzu-Nzu (eh-ph-ooh-zz-nn-ooh-zz-nn)

*Storm - Zhee-Aum-Phe-Nzu-Aum (eehzz-moo-ah-eh-ph-
ooh-zz-nn-moo-ah)*

Strength - Phe-Aum-Nzu (eh-ph-moo-ah-ooh-zz-nn)

Strike – Iuoq (ee-you-ok)

Strong – Vipu (vee-poo)

Subconscious mind –Takama (tah-ka-ah-ma)

Success - Tuu-Aum-Nzu (oot-moo-ah-ooh-zz-nn)

*Sun - Nzu-Phe-Phe-Hmu (ooh-zz-nn-eh-ph-eh-ph-you-
mmh-ha)*

Sun – Sha (shah)

Sun (power in the sun) Aya (I-yah)

Supreme – Inuwa (ee-new-wa)

Surround – Niha (nee-ha)

Sword - Zhee-Hmu-Aum-Shki (eehzz-you-mmh-ha-moo-ah-eek-hss)

Tablets – Iwazal (ee-wa-zal)

Take – Yanoto (ya-no-toh)

Tear – Weruh (weh-roo)

Telepathy – Xihe (shee-huh)

Tell – Sanuko (sa-new-ko)

Territory – Tahso (ta-so)

Terror – Upulu (you-poo-loo)

Testimony – Kehsu (kay-soo)

The/Thy – Uli (you-lee)

Thief – Sarra (sah-rah)

Thigh – Zohpa (zo-pa)

Thinking - Hmu-Bnhu-Tuu-Phe (you-mmh-ha-whoo-nn-bee-oot-eh-ph)

Thirst – Sah (sa)

Three – Tuu (oot)

Three - Bnhu-Zhee-Shki-Tuu (whoo-nn-bee-eehzz-eek-hss-oot)

Through – Xiezhi (zhay-ee-zee)

Thought –Minuk (me-nook)

Thoughts – Shenuk (she-nook)

Thunder - Zhee-Tuu-Aum-Shki (eehzz-oot-moo-ah-eek-hss)

Time - Tuu-Shki-Tuu-Aum (oot-eek-hss-oot-moo-ah)

To – De (deh)

Today - Shki-Tuu-Tuu-Zhee (eek-hss-oot-oot-eehzz)

Tomb – Kaqo (ka-ko)

Toward - Hmu-Zhee-Bnhu-Tuu (you-mmh-ha-eehzz-whoo-nn-bee-oot)

Tower – Lohuto (lo-hoo-toh)

Transform - Hmu-Tuu-Tuu-Shki (you-mmh-ha-oot-oot-eek-hss)

Transform - Shki-Phe-Tuu-Nzu (eek-hss-eh-ph-oot-ooh-zz-nn)

Transformation - Hmu-Shki-Aum (you-mmh-ha-eek-hss-moo-ah)

Treasure – Baddoh (baa-doe)

Treat – Avoo (ah-voo)

Tree - Shki-Phe-Phe-Nzu (eek-hss-eh-ph-eh-ph-ooh-zz-nn)

Triangle - *Nzu-Phe-Nzu-Tuu (ooh-zz-nn-eh-ph-ooh-zz-nn-oot)*

Tribute – *Bwato (beh-wa-toe)*

True – *Iwu (ee-woo)*

Try – *Dohuyo (doh-hoo-yo)*

Tunnel – *Pahsul (pa-sool)*

Turn – *Onev (oh-nev)*

Turned – *Usema (yuse-mah)*

Twelve – *Zhee-Aum (eehzz-moo-ah)*

Two – *Aum (moo-ah)*

Uncle – *Lehiya (leh-ee-ya)*

Unclean – *Sogwa (sog-wah)*

Uncover – *Bahew (ba-whoo)*

Underneath - *Phe-Tuu-Nzu (eh-ph-oot-ooh-zz-nn)*

Understand/Understanding – *Lil (lel)*

Union – *Selu (say-loo)*

Unity – *Pachamama (pah-cha-mama)*

Until – *Akasu (ah-ka-soo)*

Unto – Milda (mill-da)

Unveiled - Tuu-Shki-Bnhu (oot-eek-hss-whoo-nn-bee)

Unworthy – Jozaw (jo-zaw)

Upper – Wanuh (wa-new)

Upright – Fhwa (ph-wah)

Uranus – Lozaw (low-zaw)

Urge – Tuhok (too-hoke)

Us - Aum-Phe-Shki (moo-ah-eh-ph-eek-hss)

Use – Ipok (ee-poke)

Used – Rewah (ree-wah)

Utensil – Unuto (you-new-toh)

☉

Valuable – Wahel (wa-heyl)

Value – Jehta (jay-tah)

Vanity – Nulosh (new-lo-sh)

Variety – Tsudoh (tsew-doe)

Various – Oohl (uhl)

Verses – Duhi (doo-ee)

Very – Udohi (you-do-hee)

Vicinity – Tuu-Zhee-Lewhu (oot-eehzz-ooh-wel)

Victim – Atsi (aht-see)

Victory – Dunto (dune-toh)

Vessel – Hu (whoo)

Venus - zhee-aum-phe-tuu (eehzz-moo-ah-eh-ph-oot)

Venus (dragon power) – Viyah (vee-yah)

Vertical – Su (soo)

Victory – Uti (you-tee)

View – Elzoha (el-zo-ha)

Village – Basono (ba-so-no)

Violence – Nahdu (na-doo)

Violent – Nahdool (na-duel)

Virtue – Dhatri (tha-tree)

Vision – Issow (iss-sow)

Visit – Paqz (pa-qzz)

Visited – Ugipa (you-gee-pa)

Visiting – Pzio (peh-zee-oh)

Visitor/Visitors – Pzo (peh-zoh)

Visits – Pzaq (peh-zack)

Vital – Lkis (lil-kiss)

Voice - Aum-Tuu-Nzu (moo-ah-oot-ooh-zz-nn)

Vortex - Nzu-Zhee (ooh-zz-nn-eehzz)

Wait - Phe-Tuu-Nzu (eh-ph-oot-ooh-zz-nn)

Walk – Mafdet (maff-deht)

Wall – Doro (doh-row)

Want – Wanz (wah-nzz)

Want (to desire) – Menos (meh-nos)

War - Zhee-Bnhu-Tuu (eehzz-whoo-nn-bee-oot)

Warrior – Zwatoh (zz-wah-toh)

Watcher - Zwatoh (zz-wah-toh)

Water - Aum-Nzu-Phe-Bnhu (moo-ah-ooh-zz-nn-eh-ph-whoo-nn-bee)

Way – Tz (tss)

We - Bnhu-Phe-Tuu (whoo-nn-bee-eh-ph-oot)

Weak – Aejo (ah-ee-jo)

Weakness - Tuu-Aum-Nzu (oot-moo-ah-ooh-zz-nn)

Wealth - Zhee-Bnhu-Aum (eehzz-whoo-nn-bee-moo-ah)

Weapon – Iskaho (iss-ka-ho)

Weep – Ako (ah-ko)

Well – Uhr (you-her)

Went – Zsi (zz-see)

West – Ahzogo (ah-zo-go)

What - Bnhu-Hmu (whoo-nn-bee-you-mmh-ha)

White – Tuu (oot)

Why - Hmu-Tuu-Tuu (you-mmh-ha-oot-oot)

Wide – Kuwo (koo-who)

Wife – Yah (yah)

Wild – Rhunis (rue-niz)

Will - Shki-Tuu-Nzu (eek-hss-oot-ooh-zz-nn)

Wind – Melek (meh-lek)

Wine – Iskaro (iss-ka-roh)

Wing – Kapu (ka-poo)

Wise – Zemu (zeh-moo)

With – Ishtar (ish-tar)

Within – Oneto (oh-neh-toh)

Without – Kaatakilla (kah-ah-ta-kill-la)

Witness – Sehbimo (seh-bee-mo)

Wolf - Shki-Zhee-Tuu (eek-hss-eehzz-oot)

Womb - Phe-Lewhu-Phe (eh-ph-ooh-wel-eh-ph)

Wood – Idu (ee-doo)

Word - Aum-Hmu (moo-ah-you-mmh-ha)

Work - Luhw (loo-whew)

Worker – Lulu (loo-loo)

World - Shki-Tuu-Zhee (eek-hss-oot-eehzz)

World – Arzir (ar-zeer)

Worry – Nanweu (nan-weigh)

Yard – Suti (soo-tee)

Yards – Iyut (ee-voot)

Year - Zhee-Aum-Bnhu (eehzz-moo-ah-whoo-nn-bee)

Yellow – Kopoh (ko-po)

Yes - Tuu-Shki-Tuu (oot-eek-hss-oot)

Yes – Vv (vev)

Yesterday – Svhi (sev-hee)

Yet – Gila (gee-la)

You - Phe-Tuu-Zhee (eh-ph-oot-eehzz)

Young – -Seho (she-ho)

Young Men – Duha (doo-ha)

Young Woman – Duho (doo-ho)

Zeal – Pvdha (pev-dha)

Zealous – Ldilo (led-ee-lo)

Zebra – Erohu (eh-ro-hu)

Zenith (point of zenith) – Napah (na-pah)

What is Ninzuwu?

The Art of Ninzuwu is an ethno-spiritual tradition that is founded upon the cultivation of a state of awareness known as Ninzuwu (pronounced nen-zoo-woo). Although it is often associated with Shinto practice, due to many of its rites where the Kami are invoked, Ninzuwu is a culture all to its own.

The term Ninzuwu derives from the Vasuh language, spoken by natives of the said culture, and has no English equivalent. According to The Yi Jing Apocrypha of Genghis Khan, Ninzuwu is defined as *"The Magicians of the Yi Jing,"* or *one who appears as an embodiment of change.*

A Ninzuwu understands that our culture is not of recent invention, but is an extension of an invisible "secret" society, of which the tengu (Ninzuwu proper) and Ryugujo (Dragon Palace, ruled by Owatatsumi-no-Mikoto) are a part.

Many of those living today, who identify themselves as Ninzuwu, are descendants of those existing in the Dragon Palace. Our work involves preserving our culture, language, our understanding of life, and enjoying being alive, always thankful for having our knowledge.

The esoteric teachings of our culture we use to for self-transformation, and to also dispel fear and negative energy in this world. We accept newcomers and those willing to learn these methods, as an aid to preserve the will of the greater good. Our fundamental teachings are recorded in a book entitled The Ivory Tablets of the Crow. Other important texts are The Armor of Amaterasu Ohkami, The Yi Jing Apocrypha of Genghis Khan, and Ame-no-Ukihashi: The Ancient Martial Art of the Ninzuwu.

The Art of Ninzuwu was rediscovered shortly after December 21, 2012 by a shaman named Messiah'el Bey, along with a spiritualist from Argentina named Rafael Barrio. Prior to rediscovering the Art of Ninzuwu, Bey had undergone initiations in Sumerian mysticism, Simon Necronomicon, and Sect Shinto.

Bey had studied Sumerian mysticism and its shamanic practices for over 15 years before entering the world of Shinto. His knowledge of Shinto came from his studies with Toshu Fukami and the Worldmate Organization.

Bey had took a sabbatical from his work in order to spend time in self-observation and give some reflection to the instruction he received from his late mentor, who was a direct spiritual descendant of Gurdjieff. It was during this time that Bey received a revelation (Kamigakari) from Toyotama-Hime-no-Mikoto and later from Ame-o-Ukihashi-Hime-no-Mikoto, the latter being an ancient goddess who was no longer worshipped and became identified as Yukionna. These revelations gave Bey insights into a whole spiritual paradigm that includes, a calendar, language, martial arts, and a shamanic system in less than two years. This is also coupled with scores of articles, animated presentations, and many other things that serve as an aid to the Ninzuwu community.

One unique feature about the Art of Ninzuwu is that is comes with no gurus, or egos. Everyone is equal to everyone else. Our ethnicity, in the literal sense, is one based on spirit and not flesh. Here are a few principles, concerning the Art of Ninzuwu that can be gleamed from our website.

1. The Art of Ninzuwu is an ancient metaphysical technology that traces its origins back to the Oriental fraternities of shamans existing during the Jomon period. Its practices are founded in the science of Nyarzir, historically known as Ryūjin Shinkō (竜神信仰), used for the spiritual advancement of the world and the cultivation of the individual. The use of such technology for purposes of self-glorification is strictly forbidden.

2. The term "god" should not be associated with the Creator, nor defined as such. The term "god" is a title of an entity that exists within a hierarchy of beings and has nothing to do with the Creator.

3. Race is the religion of the New World Order. People who sincerely believe in "race" and advocate the categorization of the human family by means of such are evil and mentally-ill in the eyes of The Art of Ninzuwu. The true definition of race

is one's astrological sign, which all physical characteristic fall under. It is for this reason that practitioners of The Art of Ninzuwu have created a distinct ethnic identity for themselves and have dismissed all human categorization based on "racial features" as a form of mental illness.

4. The Art of Ninzuwu does not support criminal activity of any kind. Anyone seeking membership into our culture while engaging in criminal activities will be excommunicated and reported to the authorities. Crime is a disease that can only be cured through the use of spiritual technology.

5. Within all forms of life is an aspect of the source of all things, which we define as love. It is through the cultivation of the Art of Ninzuwu that this state of enlightenment in love can be achieved.

6. The Art of Ninzuwu is an ancient mystical science of self-transformation. Today, it is heavily associated with Shinto and Yi Jing Sorcery, but is historically known as Ryūjin Shinkō (竜神信仰). The Art of Ninzuwu's mission is to ensure the survival of Ninzuwu culture, along with the divine principles that it embodies.

7. While we respect individuals from all religious paths, practitioners of the Art of Ninzuwu enjoy a non-religious status. The spiritual practices of Ninzuwu should not be confused with religion and its separatist ideologies.

If you would like to receive further information about the Art of Niznuwu, or are interested in our culture, please feel free to send us an email at artofninzuwu@gmail.com

The Mystery of the Sumerianc Kings

Modern scholars are often baffled as to why the ancient Sumerians kings counted one year of rulership as 3,600 years. Yet at the same time, many of these same scholars are aware of the fact that these Sumerian kings, through the Sacred Marriage Rite received the "Power of Anu." The number of Anu is sixty and this is the power that was given over to the Kings of Sumer during the Sacred Marriage Rite. The Kings of Sumer, being 60, would now enter each zodiac sign, of which there are twelve, and pass through the five elements of each sign. Sixty times sixty elements, produced by the five elements in each zodiac sign, equals 3,600. The power of Anu is an allotrope of carbon with 60 atoms in each molecule.

ABOUT THE AUTHOR

Messiah'el Bey (also known as Warlock Asylum) is a Ninzuwu and prominent advocate of its culture. He conducts Ninzuwu ceremonies, healing sessions, and various workshops on Ninzuwu-Shinto practices. Bey has written a wide variety of works on Ninzuwu culture, and other aspects of mysticism and esoteric practices found in ancient China, Japan, and Mesopotamia.

Made in the USA
Middletown, DE
08 March 2025

72423345R00138